Communing
With the Spirit of Your
Unborn Child

A Practical Guide
to Intimate Communication
With Your Unborn or
Infant Child

By
Dawson Church

Published by

Aslan Publishing
830 Castro Street
San Leandro, CA 94577
USA

Church, Dawson, 1956-
    Communing with the spirit of your unborn child: a practical
guide to intimate communication with your unborn or infant
child / by Dawson Church.
    p.   cm.
    Bibliography: p.
    ISBN 0-944031-15-3 (pbk.): $8.95
    1. Spiritualism. 2. Fetus–Miscellanea. 3. Prenatal
influences–Miscellanea. 4. Parent and child–Miscellanea.
I. Title.
BF 1311.F47C48   1988
133.9'1–dc19   88-21548
                                                    CIP

© 1988, Dawson Church

Cover Illustration by Charles Waltmire
Book Production by Brenda Plowman
Printed in USA by Specialty Web
10 9 8 7 6 5 4 3 2 1
First Edition

This book is dedicated to

Lloyd Arthur Meeker

*whose passionate love illuminated
the path of spiritual education for many,
and*

William Martin Alleyne Cecil,
7th Marquess of Exeter

*whose conscious expression
of the living spirit of truth was confirmed
by the absolute manifestation of it in his living*

Acknowledgements

Many thanks to all those whose love and encouragement have meant so much to us personally, and have contributed to the development of this book: Nancy Bauer, Paula Begoun, Ken and Sherry Carey and the Spirit of Greenwood Forest, Michael Exeter, Bill Hurst, Barbara Ingber, Jerry Kaiser, Kim Koenig, Linda Kramer, John and Nancy Krysko, Adele Leone, Rupert Maskell, Libby McGreevey, Cliff Penwell, Leonard Perillo, Roxanne Potter, Darlene Ravin, Sanaya Roman and Duane Packer, Bill Stroh, Charles Waltmire. Photographs by Michael Fong; author portrait by Marc Raboy.

Contents

Introduction

This book came as quite a surprise. One clear winter night, standing gazing at the stars, sensing the stillness of the redwood trees on the remote mountain where we lived, the book sprang to mind in its entirety: title, outline, approach, everything.

Although I was extremely busy, working twelve to fifteen hours a day, I dropped everything and started typing. Seven intense days later, the manuscript was complete.

My partner and I were four months pregnant at the time. I had been doing "radiance exercises" with our unborn child, similar to some of those in the book, ever since we consciously knew of conception.

Long before there was any physical bulge to demonstrate the baby's presence, we developed a marked spiritual bulge! I began to sense the child's spirit very strongly. This experience became more and more specific and a close communion with the spirit of the unborn child developed. I became aware of the the potential of this link. We could develop a relationship with the incoming spirit long before birth and ease its transition into the world.

As the frequency and depth of my communication with the child grew, I began to sense the character and intent of this spirit in a very specific way. I began to sense the identity of this being I was helping welcome into the earth, and the purpose for which it had chosen to incarnate.

That night under the stars, I felt the spirit of this incoming one very close. In that state of still communion, it seemed I was tapping into the mind of the baby. In its mind I sensed, among other things, the desire to communicate to other parents the possibility of conscious prenatal contact with the fetus. The spirit of this baby wanted to explicitly lay out for other parents the practical steps they can take to get in touch with their children in the period of stillness that precedes birth.

Beyond that, <u>Communing With the Spirit of Your Unborn Child</u> has a broader message that applies to every person on earth, not just parents-to-be. That message is that it is possible for us to be fully healed, to be fully who we are, that we can at *any* age assume the perspective of the eternal universal child, full of wonder, awe and innocence. We can move through the world, move through our lives with grace, unafraid, releasing a constant stream of blessing and healing to everything and everyone around us. It is never too late to be a child! No matter what our physical age is, a small but radical change of perspective enables us to see, through a child's eyes, a fresh, magical world, full of the glory and beauty of newness.

What you will read is what I understand of the message I became aware of. I wrote the words pretty much as I sensed them in the moment. Whenever I have been stuck for words, all I have had to do is listen to the voices that spring from the silence within.

If any one of us ever loses the child that ought to dwell eternally in our heart, all we have to do is be silent, and deeply listen. We will find the fountain of youth springing from within the roots of our own being. Its dynamic flow has the power to renew and reinvigorate reality, past, present and future.

1

The Universe is Speaking To Us

In recent times we have come to understand that our planet functions as a living organism. It has a circulatory system in the oceans, clouds, rain and rivers; a respiratory system in the great tropical forests, and all the other characteristics of a living creature. In this planetary whole, humankind plays the role of the global brain, a communicator and integrator of information. Humans are the conscious component of Earth.

But up to this point, humankind has not been in position to fulfill this responsibility to the whole. Functioning out of a paradigm of self-centeredness, acting as though we alone mattered, humankind has been destructive. Our species has been like a diseased organ, preying on the whole organism in order to gain those things we short-sightedly consider to be in our own interest.

We have acted more like planetary "rogue cells," a cancer, than a life-enhancing organ of conscious dominion. We have seen only our selves, ignoring the intricately designed integrity of the ecological context in which we live. Our actions, springing from this diseased premise, threaten to destroy our planetary host and ourselves along with it.

But this cycle of deviance from the larger rhythm of life has almost run its course. Any pattern of function that is at cross-purposes with the whole must in the long run be futile. It can have no end other than exhaustion and extinction. This temporary, myopic mutant of planetary man, Homo Ignoramus, has had his day, and is about to be laid to an unlamented rest.

As the new day dawns in human consciousness, and New Man prevails, living in harmony with the planetary whole, a radical transformation takes place. Humankind finds its place in creation. This second Renaissance is the defining watershed of planetary history. Children of the future may well ask: "How was it possible for people of the twentieth century to kill each other?" Such actions will seem as inconceivable to them as the rack, garotte and thumbscrew are to us.

Life works in synchronized harmony throughout the cosmos. Only in this one, curious, deviant world do we find the dominant species creating conditions which are inimical to its own survival and the survival of the whole. The universe has given us gentle reminders of reality from time to time, in the persons of great teachers who have come to call our memory back to the path of planetary integration.

We have had just as many great teachers as we, as a species, could assimilate. Each prophet of the global path has brought the power of alignment with life into the realm of human options. Homo Ignoramus has historically attempted to dilute these messages by encapsulating them in a shroud of religious dogma, rendering the message impotent by deifying the messenger and ignoring the message.

Through the immortal words of these great ones, the patterns of life have been prodding our reluctant human consciousness, knocking at the door of our awareness for centuries. Our ability to deafen our ears is weakening. At this point in our species' evolution, we are collectively ripe for a shift in our underlying assumptions about the nature of the cosmos and our position within it. The unsustainability of the old way of doing things is becoming apparent to even the most intransigent.

From Chaos to Cosmos

A new thing is happening on planet Earth. A transition is taking place from the old way of doing things to a new way. The old way is characterized by unconsciousness: unconsciousness of the way that the patterns and rhythms of life operate in the universe.

The new way is characterized by a conscious desire to be at one with the rhythms of cosmic and personal nature, to fit in with the larger scheme of things. Paradoxically, it is by fitting in to the whole that we discover the fulness of our individuality.

If we bring the innate order of the cosmos into practical manifestation by living lives which are true to its principles, we both fulfill our maximum potential as individuals and bring our personal worlds into the sphere of influence of the life-order. It is our day-to-day living that has the potential to link the part with the whole, the mundane with the sublime, the ordinary with the transcendent.

To teach us these lessons, the beings responsible for the spiritual well-being of the planet, and this includes the true, inner, angelic nature of each one of us, are supplying us with a huge number of learning aids. Some of them are metaphysical "toys," through which by simple play we learn some of the basic patterns of the cosmos. Others are very powerful instruments of personal transformation which must be handled with care. We see, for example, widespread popular interest in channeling, crystals and so on. Psychospiritual tools have gone from back-alley curiosities to become big business, with big profits. Good teachers, bad teachers, and many varieties of indifferent teachers abound. Books, films, print and electronic media are "catching on" to the spiritual revolution. It has reached the highest levels of government.

It has even reached the organized religions, traditionally the first to reject and the last to accept spiritual regeneration. Fundamentalists, traditionalists, orthodoxes, modernists and reformists are finding a kinship in their hearts to the teachings of their faith. It is reaching into the heart of every religion on the globe, subversively using the very teachings at their cores, long buried under the graveclothes of liturgical chores, to revitalize them.

Teachers Old and New

For the purposes of renewal, a whole new order of beings is incarnating on Earth, choosing to assume physical forms in order to assist this species-awakening. They are not subject to the limitations of the last generations. They are pushing at the boundaries of all cultural forms.

In the past, such exceptional beings donned human guise only occasionally, in order to keep the whole human experiment on track. No age could tolerate too many of them, for the reaction to them by the old, stuck human habits of thinking would have been too great. The old way would have risen up, had the light shone too brightly, and tried to smother it from the very face of the earth. This, if successful, would have doomed the entire species to a swift death. The universe in its wisdom gave man no more light than he could handle in ages past. Any more, and we would have been blinded and fallen into the abyss.

But now the quantity of light is increasing exponentially. Enough human "faithful ones" have remained steadfast over the last few centuries to allow a steady pattern of welcome to be established for the light. It is now unstoppable, like the brilliance of a fiery gem bursting through the seams of an outworn cloth bag.

To accomplish this, life is sending us great teachers. But we are not receiving just one Moses, one Gautama, one Lao-Tzu per epoch. They are coming into human form by the dozens. They are coming into the human forms of our children, our infants, our unborns, our fetuses, our yet-to-be borns. They are coming to speed up the process of planetary evolution.

If we teach our children using even the most advanced lessons of yesterday, we will miss the mark. The lessons they need to learn are radically different. The lessons they have come to teach are vital, and must not be obstructed by the old forms of so-called education. The most enlightened of the nineteenth-century educational approaches are inappropriate to a twentieth century child. To use them is like hitching an ox wagon to a bullet train.

The most advanced, enlightened education of the late twentieth century will be just as inapplicable to the twenty-first century child. How do we as parents then take responsibility for stewarding them, guiding them? The most important education we can give them is instruction in "the perennial philosophy," the enduring truths that the great masters have exemplified for us through the ages. If we as parents are able to represent the ways of life to them, and ground their minds and hearts in resonant connection with universal truths, the rest of education can take care of itself.

When it comes to specialized knowledge, perhaps they will become their own teachers, designing curricula for themselves that are far beyond our ability to comprehend. I used to think, when I was a child, that adults didn't understand me. "They don't know what it's like to be a child," I thought, "but when I grow up, I'll remember. I won't treat my children the way they treated me. I'll treat them the way I would like to be treated now."

However, if I try to treat my children the way I wish I had been treated as a child, I will be trying to confine them to an ancient, creaking conceptual straightjacket. In the thirty-year gap between me as a child, and the children of the future, the world has changed. The universe has moved on. Those things that were true for me then belong to the ox wagon stage of human development compared to where we as a race have moved in the interim.

Gifts From The Stars

The universe is gifting the earth with souls appropriate for this stage of our development as a species. It is not sending us the kind of souls that were required in the nineteenth century, or the ninth century. It is sending us souls of the twenty-first century, harbingers of the light. Look into the eyes of a newborn baby. There is a wisdom there, a connection with universal source that is utterly present. Our outer physical forms have not changed much – yet. They will change in the future, I suspect. But though the outer forms have not changed, the inner spirit of the newborn is very different. Light streams from them.

As parents our responsibility is to create a spiritual and physical climate that will allow for the maximum shining of that light. In the bad old days, society tried in every conceivable way to smother that light after birth. The child was pushed through a process ludicrously entitled "education." The child was indoctrinated into something called a religion, the chief effect of which was to stifle the child's inherent knowing of God. This was done either by burying that innate gnosis in a stultifying morass of pointless ritual, or by stuffing theology down a resistant throat till it was regurgitated as unthinking atheism.

The new parent is, instead, a sacred nurturer of the light of the newborn. *All* parenting is sacred parenting. There is no parenting that is not inherently a sacred act. The parent has the responsibility of finding the means to allow an increase of the inner being of the child. For although the inherent potential is there, it is not conscious yet, and the parent is (hopefully) conscious. The sacred parent does nothing to stand in the way of that potential. The sacred parent allows the light that comes to focus in the child to shine fully through them, and kindle the unconscious light in them. Every parent has an unceasing responsibility to the child to be the light, to represent the light.

This book assumes that a parent can make contact with the unborn child on the spiritual level, and establish a useful channel of connection with that child to allow increased bonding and understanding. This process will undoubtedly deepen the spiritual understanding of the parents as well.

Reinventing Earth

As these new teachers incarnate among us, they bring to the mass subconscious of humanity a measure of understanding and education in the processes of life. At present we are seeing an explosion of these global beings incarnating as newborns. This is the primary means through which the Universe is preparing our planet for the advent of a new age. The Universe is speaking to us in the language of the future, and the words of the new language are our babies.

These newborns are a gift to us from the stars. They are the people of tomorrow. They will not be living their lives by the rules by which we live, our parents lived, or our grandparents lived. God is reinventing the Earth, and with it man is being remade in His image.

Chapter

2

The Welcome

At the instant of conception, a world is born, full of new potentials and possibilities. The potential for rapid, accelerated growth is present, not only in the fetus, but also in the spiritual understanding of the parents. At some point after conception, the couple will consciously know they are pregnant. It is not unheard of for the woman to know intuitively that conception has taken place immediately after it occurs. But at whatever point it reveals itself, at some moment there is the realization: "We are pregnant!"

This may be a long-hoped-for event. Or it may seem like an unforeseen calamity! Whichever it is, spiritual parenting demands of us that we have a very particular attitude at the instant of conscious knowing of conception.

This attitude is one of welcome. If our first flush of

feeling is one of panic, of upset, of rejection, of dismay, this will set a pattern which will remain for the development of the child. If the feeling is one of rejoicing, of acceptance, of welcome, this creates a wonderful beam of energy on which the soul may travel in.

The child knows whether it is wanted or not. Just because the outer form of the child's mind is not yet developed does not mean that a certain level of knowing is not there. In spirit we know all things. We know things that are so far beyond the comprehension of our conscious mind, that, were it to endeavor to understand them, it would go insane. The outer conscious mind simply cannot encompass the things of spirit. In spirit all things are known. When our identity is in spirit, things are known to us far beyond the scope of the perception of our conscious mind.

So our responsibility as parents begins the moment of conscious knowledge of conception. We may feel panic, dismay or uncertainty, but this our opportunity to transcend these feelings. Whatever cartwheels our emotions might do at the instant of conscious knowing, we keep our spirit steady, radiating welcome and acceptance of a new soul.

This is the first great blessing we can offer our baby. It is the first spiritual gift we can give. More will follow, but if the first gift is fitly given, it establishes a pattern for the giving of everything else.

We give thanks that a great spirit has consented to bless the physical form of our child with its presence, that it has chosen to incarnate through us. We give thanks that our love has provided the vehicle for the induction of a spirit that has come to bless the earth.

Easing the Transition

A soul's transition to the physical plane is made easier if they know that the parents of the child through whom they are choosing to incarnate plan to do all that they can to make that soul's full manifestation possible.

When you go to visit a friend or relative, how do you view the upcoming visit? If you know that you will be given a royal welcome, that everything possible will be done by the ones who are receiving you to make you feel at home, accepted, at peace, you will look forward to it. If you know that they will be grumpy, preoccupied with their own selfish concerns, unable to be conscious of the larger world around them, you will likely view the coming visit as an ordeal.

The same thing is true at the soul level. If we can make the spirit of our baby feel welcomed, it will affect the entire incarnation. This is why at the instant of conscious knowing of conception, it is vital to roll out the welcome mat in consciousness!

Shedding Heredity and Environment

What about a situation in which the earthly parents are not happy to learn that they are pregnant? What about a case in which the parents don't want the child – view it as an imposition, as a nuisance, as a disruption?

Sometimes a soul that is placed in such a position by the prospective parents will check out: simply not incarnate. This may mean abortion, spontaneous or induced, stillbirth, etc. Or the baby may decide to come in anyway. The incoming child can overcome many things. Many of us may have had parents who were ambivalent or even hostile to our birth. If the soul believes it can accomplish its mission despite a lack of allies, it may come on in anyway.

Spirit can overcome all things. It can take the most nasty, twisted, problematic origins and turn them into something beautiful. We don't have to remain turkeys if we know that we can fly as eagles. If we trust our inner sensing of our divine potential, even if we get NO reinforcement for this belief from the outside world or anyone in it, our knowledge of spirit can make our inner beauty manifest. Our dreams of our potential can come true. We do not have to remain limited by anything. **We can always transcend our background.** In actual fact, our spirit has already transcended it. As soon as we get in touch with that reality and become one with spirit, we transcend our background too.

This reality is ever present. If you as parents did not give thanks at first, but have come later in the pregnancy process to an understanding of the imperatives of spiritual parenting, give thanks now, now that you have come into this knowledge. This process of giving thanks for conception is possible at any time. And the flood of blessing that is released when parents become thankful for their children can flood retroactively backwards in time to heal wounds present from the time of conception.

Even if that blessing was not there in linear time, it can be implanted in spiritual time. Spiritual time does not respect the boundaries of linear time. There are no limits to spirit. When it is given free reign, when it is allowed to flood into a situation, it overflows backwards in time to bless us from the point of conception. In the

14

enlightened moment, every other moment is enlightened. In the moment of enlightenment, every other instant of our lives, past, present and future, is bathed in light. It overflows to everyone we know, everyone we have ever known, every one we will know in the "future."

You may have parents that never gave thanks for your incarnation. But as you allow thankfulness to flood your being, you bless your own past. In this way you allow spirit to be your true parent, touching your own birth with the hand of healing.

Welcoming the Unknown

The following Meditation may be done either to welcome in the spirit of your unborn child, or to welcome your own spirit now, which will welcome your spirit all the way to the time of your physical conception–however many years ago that may have been.

Make yourself comfortable, in a quiet, darkened room. Make sure you will not be disturbed for about 45 minutes. If you have the tape of <u>Communing With the Spirit of Your Unborn Child</u> (use order form in back of book) you can use this. If not, either read the Meditation to yourself, or record it on a tape and then play it back to yourself. You may play some background music at low volume, something that is not distracting. If you have learned a specific meditative technique, meditate for a while before you begin the Meditation. You know your own patterns and habits. Do whatever is necessary to make yourself completely relaxed.

•••••

First Meditation

Close your eyes. Breathe deeply. With each out-breath, visualize all the things that you worry about, that occupy your mind, that distract you from the present moment, flowing out of your body with the breath.

Let your breathing become regular, and with each breath, expel a little more of the tension till your body is completely relaxed and your mind is still.

Breathe out, exhaling all the old, stale air from your lungs. Relax, and allow pure, clean, fresh air to be drawn back in. Breathe out and in several times in this manner. With each outbreath, feel the tension leave your body. As you breathe in, feel the fresh air streaming over your brain and mind, washing out all the pre-occupations in your head. Let all your concerns, your worries, fade into the background. Let the cool, white, incoming air soothe your frustrations, smoothing over the rough patches in your life.

Visualize your body as being filled with green energy. This green energy is all the stored tensions that have been retained in your muscles and organs. See how this energy fills all of your limbs. Start at your feet. With each outbreath, feel the energy flowing out of your feet with the breath. Take as many outbreaths as required to clear out this green fluid from every nook and cranny of your feet.

Then go up your calves, thighs, pelvis, and work your way up. Take as much time as required to make sure that each part is completely relaxed. Turn off the tape until you have had time to release the tensions in

16

every part of your torso.

When you have completely cleared your shoulders of this fluid green energy, and each part of your body feels completely limp, see the energy that fills your head. Start at the back of your skull, and begin to expel it with each breath. Keep going till even the smallest cavities in your head have been emptied of the green energy, and no tension or tightness remains.

Finally, empty your neck and mouth of the fluid, and feel how completely relaxed your body has become.

Now let your attention review each part of your body again, to see if there are still any remaining pockets of the tension-energy. Find the subtle places where tension is still lingering, and allow it to flow easily out of you on the current of your breath.

Now as you breathe in, imagine a bright, glowing white substance, like mist. It is full of energy and life. Breathe it in, and feel it move to every part of your body, rejuvenating and soothing your muscles, your emotions, your mind. Let it smooth over all the bumps of worry and anxiety in your experience. Forget about all the problems you usually deal with, and feel your whole being invigorated by the experience of peace and vitality that it brings.

Think back to your first meeting with a child you really loved. It may be a brother or sister, or the child of a friend, or a child you only met once, but who filled you with joy. Whatever child it is, just remember how wonderful you felt being with that child: how beautiful that child was, how innocent, how fresh, how inspiring. Think of all the positive things you felt about that child. Remember all the feelings you felt when you were

17

around that child. Give thanks for the presence of that child on earth, wherever it may be right now.

Now picture the soul of that child. See the essences of spirit that came to focus in that child. Picture the great and profound presence that underlays that child's physical form. Blend with that presence. Give thanks for that presence.

Now picture that child's face blending into your own face, the face of yourself as an infant. See yourself as full of wonder as you remember that child-being. See all the potential in yourself that you saw in that magical child. Hold this strong image of yourself blending into all that was fine and perfect in the ideal child. Feel the great soul that is you coming in to that little body. Feel that magnificent soul fill that body with vibrant light, so that every cell sings with thankfulness. Feel the presence of God touching the child's body all around, protecting it from harm and hurt.

Now imagine yourself as a younger child. Get younger and younger each moment until you see yourself at birth, and keep going. Feel what it was like to be in the womb. Feel how safe and snug it is, how secure you feel, how protected you feel from all harm. Enjoy floating in the fluid environment of this quiet place.

Keep on getting younger. Get smaller, as you go back in time to the first cells that were you, till you are only one cell. Then, from above, a bright light bursts in above you, a streak of lightning filled with love and purpose. It is spirit incarnating in your form. It fills you with purpose. Suddenly you feel you are heavenly, angelic. Experience yourself as part of both worlds: the cell, earthly, and the spirit, divine. Feel the exquisite *tension of this dual nature.*

Feel your soul giving thanks for the priceless opportunity to be incarnate. Your soul has been disincarnate for many years. Now at last it has the chance to be creative in form on earth. And its first act of creation is to create you, the proto-fetus! You are the first creative act of love made manifest! You are filled with excitement and thankfulness.

Now, with this priceless knowledge firmly fixed in your awareness, this bliss of divinity, go forward in time again, as your cells grow and develop into a baby, then to birth. Bring this divine light to your own birth. Bless your birth with the wisdom and compassion of your own spirit.

Then move along to your childhood. Think of the wonderful times that you had, the achievements you were proud of. Let your divinity shine through those moments.

Now think of the worst incident you can remember as a child: the thing which terrified you the most; the most traumatic thing you experienced. Feel the way it felt. Re-experience all the agony.

Now bring your light, the light of spirit, to that situation. Comfort that grieving, ailing child. Bring the full force of your divinity to bear. Let the child feel your presence, feel that everything is all right. Smooth away the tears. Wash away the grief in the flowing river of your love. When the child is happy and comforted, move on to another such situation. Go through the process again. Comfort and sustain the child.

As time goes on, you see your whole life in front of you, stage by stage. Wherever there was trauma, imagine yourself there, your divine self, with an endless supply of healing love. See how your soul guided your outer form to develop it to the point where you are today. Today you are able to see and actually experience the soul. This is the greatest miracle of all — that you can see and realize your oneness with your own divine self!

Your divinity is welcoming your body into manifestation. This divine presence embraces every stage of your life. It gives thanks for the miracle of your conception, birth and survival. You feel the immense sense of gratitude your soul felt at the instant of conception. You reach back and bless that instant now.

When you are ready to come back into your body, become aware of your breathing once again. Slowly become conscious of your inbreath and outbreath. Notice how relaxed your body feels, how refreshed you are. Become aware of the room you are in. As you get up and begin to move around, keep the feeling of thankfulness for being on earth with you. Keep it present with you the whole day. Let it infuse all of your activities this day.

•••••

The above Meditation is for use in preparing the consciousness of the adult who is initiating a connection with the child. Until our own attitude is right, our own heart is still, we do not have the stillness in our own hearts to allow the fulness of welcome to flow through us to the baby. It is important to clear our own inner creative field of distractions, tension and limitations, otherwise part of our attention is siphoned off into these concerns, and we are not fully available to welcome our baby.

Once we have prepared our consciousness in this way, we are "all there" and can bring our full attention to bear on greeting the spirit of the incoming child. The Second Meditation is for use after you have completed the First Meditation and focuses on the welcome itself.

The first three paragraphs of the Second Meditation are an abbreviated form of the relaxation exercise which starts off the First Meditation. If a long period (several hours) or intense activity elapses between using the two Meditations, it is useful to use the longer form of relaxation found in the First Meditation before proceeding to the Second.

•••••

Second Meditation

Close your eyes. Breathe deeply. With each out-breath, visualize all the things that you worry about, that occupy your mind, that distract you from the present moment, flowing out of your body with the breath.

Let your breathing become regular, and with each breath, expel a little more of the tension till your body is completely relaxed and your mind is still.

Now as you breathe in, imagine a bright, glowing white substance, like mist. It is full of energy and life. Breathe it in, and feel it move to every part of your body rejuvenating and soothing your muscles, your emotions, your mind. It smooths over all the bumps of worry and anxiety in your experience. Forget about all the problems you usually deal with, and feel your whole being invigorated by the experience of peace and vigor that it brings.

Hold your hand over the pregnant uterus. Feel the presence of the child within. Feel the energy that emanates from the child to your hand. Feel your own spirit radiating back to the child. Feel the interplay of appreciation between the two of you.

Picture the details of the child's body, even though it may only be a fetus a few weeks old. Picture its head, its torso, its limbs. Now picture a glowing light in the middle of its chest where its heart is. See the love that is in that heart. Your own heart starts to glow with a sympathetic resonance. Your heartbeat synchronizes with the heartbeat of the fetus.

Now picture a ray of brilliant white light reaching up from your shared glowing hearts up into the heavens. It is the beacon that will guide the spirit into the body. This is your signal to the soul that it is welcome, that you are ready and waiting for it. This brilliant light illuminates the soul's path so that it may find the child's body.

As the soul comes down the light-pathway to the body, a cloud of love and power descends. You can feel its presence. The baby can feel its presence. You feel your own body respond to the soul of the child with love and welcome. Thank the soul for choosing to incarnate. Give thanks for the role you played in making this incarnation possible.

As the soul blends with the child's body, the beam of light gradually fades and becomes less focused, until it is just a glow which surrounds the baby. With this glow of protection hovering all around the child, you become aware of your breathing once again. You feel *yourself breathing in and out, in and out, in and out. You have a tremendous sense of well-being. Your body feels refreshed and renewed.*

Return your awareness to the room you are in. The sense of thankfulness will stay with you the whole day. At any time of this day you choose, you can feel your link to the baby as a glowing white cord that connects you. Along this cord, love and blessing flow. Every time you remember the baby throughout this day, allow your sense of thankfulness, welcome and appreciation to flow along this cord.

●●●●●

It is never too late for a welcome. At whatever moment you learn to give thanks for the wonder of your own birth, for the wonder of your child's birth, you have given spirit thanks for coming into the world. As spirit is welcomed into the world it fills the world, and the world is transformed.

Chapter

3

The Womb

The womb, in a physical sense, is a place where gestation of the physical form takes place. It is a place of protection. In it, the processes that create physical life are allowed to take form unhindered. In it, a new being may grow and come into manifestation in perfect safety and security. The womb is an extraordinarily effective system for cushioning the developing fetus from the jars and shocks of the outside world. It is a safe place into which nothing can enter that does not belong in the burgeoning of physical life.

From conception to grave, the womb is probably the safest place any of us will ever be. Once we leave it, all kinds of perils threaten. We may find ourselves at the mercy of the capricious whims of an arbitrary society, whose rules are not the rules of the kingdom of life. In the womb, our innate beauty and creativity is not stifled, as it so frequently is during childhood. On the contrary, our innate perfection is free to express itself and become manifest.

Given these facts, it is no wonder that, during regressive therapies such as hypnotherapy, patients weary from study at the school of hard knocks often dream of going back to the womb. It's not the literal, physical womb that is missed so much as that *feeling* of safety.

Have you ever seen a Japanese bonsai tree? These are full-grown trees, though they may be only a foot high. They are kept small by tightly wrapping their branches with wire. Their growth is suppressed by constantly plucking out the growing tips of the branches. They are twisted into the forms deemed most pleasing by the gardener.

Inherent in each seed is the pattern of the full-grown plant. If seeds are allowed to mature without distortion, the full-grown plant reveals the beauty and glory that was potential in the seed. If, however, as the plant is growing, rocks are piled on top of it, or its developing branches are twisted and deformed by outside agents, the finished form does not reveal the full potential that existed in the seed.

This same process happens to most children. Their initiative is plucked out of them by an educational system that emphasizes rote learning, which is primarily a device to make it easy to classify large numbers of children by means of grades. Their growing forms are twisted by parental expectations, by peer pressure, by the arbitrary phobias of a mad society; by work, marriage, and all the other pressures of late twentieth century life. No wonder we look back on the womb with nostalgia. It was a precious time of unfettered growth, before the deluge of distortions suddenly hit us!

Seeing Past the Veil

Think, for a moment, of another world. This world provides the same sense of safety, of nurturing of one's growth, that the womb provided. However, in this ideal world, that protection extends one's whole life long. The whole of life is lived in a womb of love. Instead of the innate beauty of each person being distorted and blasted by the malevolent winds of the outside world, it is encouraged to grow into full bloom. Every person blossoms in their own way. No one is beaten down, denied expression, distorted by the expectations of others, or forced into the mold of a conformist culture.

This imaginary culture embodies the Spirit of the Womb. Each individual is allowed to flourish in their own way. The glorious potential of each one is unlocked. Society is enriched by the full release of each individual's special gift.

As our understanding of the process of fetal development has grown over the last few years, we have come to realize that certain sensations do get through to the womb. Prenatal psychologists have begun to turn up stories of people who, years later, remember things they could only have heard in the womb. The fetus does not abruptly begin to absorb sensory experiences once it leaves the womb. Its senses are functioning long before birth, busily receiving messages from the outside world.

As our spiritual understanding increases, we likewise come to realize that as well as being permeated by physical-level phenomena such as sound waves, the womb is permeated by spiritual and invisible forces. Emotions and thoughts can reach right through the physical flesh to touch and influence the growing child.

Vision of the Inner Eye

Because we as a culture have been concerned chiefly with the physical and outward manifestations of things, we have tended to look at everything, including birth, from that level. As we move to the next level, as we metamorphose in consciousness into Homo Spiritus, spiritual man, we become aware of the spiritual dimension, and how it underlies and permeates the physical level.

We no longer see human beings merely in terms of their outer forms. We see the inner reality of things. We no longer rely on our physical eyes as our primary source of information. We see with the eyes of spirit, often noticing subtleties far beyond the scope of our physical senses. We may see something as being so, even though our physical eyes say it is not so. When the physical eyes look at the acorn, they see only an insignificant speck of matter. Seen with the eyes of spirit, though, potential is revealed, and the glorious oak tree is evident.

We similarly become aware that the physical level of the womb is not the end of the story. It is the beginning. It is underlaid with a greater reality: The Spirit of the Womb.

The Spirit of the Womb embraces all those qualities which we associate with the physical womb: safety, security, peace, stillness, growth, protection. The Spirit of the Womb might be defined as follows: the place in which the processes of life are kept inviolate.

Every pregnant couple has the responsibility for the creation and maintenance of this spirit. It is the responsibility of the male as much as it is for the female. Looking at a pregnant couple, physical level vision would judge the woman to be the one having the womb. When we look through the eyes of spirit and become conscious of the Spirit of the Womb, we realize that both the man and the woman are responsible for carrying and maintaining the womb, undefiled.

Choosing Peace Means Not Choosing War

The man has a particular responsibility in this regard. The woman has a primary responsibility on the physical level. The man has a primary responsibility on a spiritual level. The Spirit of the Womb is a place he carries within himself, with which he exercises great care. This involves not allowing negative or destructive thoughts and emotions to enter in. Un-whole thoughts blow through the consciousness of each person, coming from our own subconscious, from the mass consciousness, from wherever. But we do not give them a home in our own form! We have the option to say **NO!** We allow them to move through us, not resisting them, but certainly not harboring them. If we harbor them we pollute the purity of the Spirit of the Womb.

For example, a man may have a persistent judgmental thought pattern with respect to his partner: "I don't like you driving with your foot on the clutch. It makes me angry!" During pregnancy, with consummate care for preserving the Spirit of the Womb, a man might care to notice such things that set him off, and not allow himself to react to them. Care is taken to develop an atmosphere of harmony, which can remain with him as the child grows up.

Those situations that grate on us the most are the very ones in which it is most important that we maintain our inner stillness. Aggravations, in fact, are life's way of telling us: "Here is an area that needs attention, in which the power of peace, harmony and joy is absent. I am telling you this so that you can change your unthinking, habitual behavior. I am telling you this so that you can cease exploding these spiritual bombs that so disturb the patterns of creative unfoldment in your own life and the lives of those around you. This irritation is my way of bringing this unhealed part of yourself to your attention, so that you may bless and heal it."

All the things that commonly arise to disturb the peace between two people in a relationship have no place during pregnancy. The Spirit of the Womb is paramount. If these angers are expressed, they are like vibratory arrows shot into the fetus. They impede the healthy spiritual development of the child.

Preserving the Spirit of the Womb is something that is done in your own mind and heart. You are choosing not to express certain behaviors that do not belong. The womb is created inside you. You maintain this place of serenity and safety in which your own spiritual potential and that of your child may grow. Control is present in the womb. Deliberation is required to maintain it. Things which do not belong in there are not kept around. It is a carefully controlled environment in which only creativity has a place. It is a place of joy, of welcome, of peace.

Becoming the Peacekeeping Force

A man is thus not without a role in creating the womb. If he is conscious of the Spirit of the Womb, if he takes responsibility for the atmosphere around his family, he is a co-creator of the safe place in which life can bloom. The soul of the child needs, during gestation, to draw together many specific vibratory factors which will be required later in life. If these invisible vibratory factors are not interfered with by stray arrows of resentment, anger or doubt and the like, the soul may construct its house of spirit without interference. If it has to battle with the uncontrolled negative emotions of the birth partners, it senses the lack of welcome.

The Spirit of the Womb is thus a sacred space in the heart and mind of the mother *and* father.

The following Exercise may be of assistance in sensing the Spirit of the Womb. Do it in a darkened, silent room, either alone or with your partner. Make yourself completely comfortable before you begin. If you have the meditation tape also entitled <u>Communing with The Spirit Of Your Unborn Child</u>, play it softly. If not, read the Exercise below onto a tape and play it back, or have your partner read it softly and gently to you.

•••••

Exercise

Feel how comfortable your body has become. Feel the rhythm of your breath as you breathe in and out. Slow your breathing gradually. As your breathing becomes slower and deeper, imagine all the tensions of the day leaving with each breath. As you breathe and breathe, your body becomes soft and limp as all the tensions leave.

Breathe out, exhaling all the old, stale air from your lungs. Relax, and allow pure, clean, fresh air to be drawn back in. Breathe out and in in this manner several times. With each outbreath, feel the tension leave your body. As you breathe in, feel the fresh air streaming over your brain and mind, washing out all preoccupations. Let all your concerns, your worries, fade into the background. Let the cool, white incoming air soothe your frustrations, smoothing over the rough patches in your life.

Visualize your body as being filled with green energy. This green energy is all the stored tensions that have been retained in your muscles and organs. See how this energy fills all of your limbs. Start at your feet. On each outbreath, feel the energy flowing out of your feet with the breath. Take as many outbreaths as required to clear out this green fluid from every nook and cranny of your feet.

Then go up your calves, thighs, pelvis, and work your way up. When you have completely cleared your shoulders of this fluid green energy, and each part of your body feels completely limp, see the energy that fills your head. Start at the back of your skull, and begin to expel it with each breath. Keep going till even the smallest cavities in your head have been emptied of the green energy, and no tension or tightness remain.

Finally, empty your neck and mouth of the fluid, and feel how completely relaxed your body has become.

Now let your attention review each part of your body again, to see if there are still any remaining pockets of the tension-energy. Find the subtle places where tension is still lingering, and allow it to flow easily out of you on the current of your breath.

Hold your hand or hands about twelve inches above the uterus. Visualize the child within. Imagine you can see clearly, using the eyes of spirit. Picture your baby's body. With your hand hovering above, you can sense what is going on in the womb. What sensations can you feel in your hand?

Now picture a bubble around your baby, extending a foot or more from the baby's body. This is the spiritual womb in which the soul is drawing together the vibrational substance which surrounds the baby as it grows. What color does it seem to be predominantly? What other colors are present? Is it moving? Pulsing? Or is it still?

Now visualize sending a current of radiant light from your hand to the bubble around the baby. Picture this stream of blessing pouring forth from you to the baby's spirit. Does the baby respond in any way? If not, fine. If it does, what does it do?

Move your hand over the surface of the bubble, touching it in each part, as you would caress a child. You are caressing the child's energy field. You are smoothing out the rough edges, and giving love and affirmation through your hand. You are welcoming this soul into the world. Let the full force of your love move through your hand. Feel the intensity of the moment increase as you pour your love out upon the child. Feel its love coming back to you, moving back to you through your hand. Feel the intensity increase as you exchange love with each other.

Sense the greatness of spirit that lies behind the baby. Give thanks to that soul for blessing this body with its presence. Give thanks for the moment of conception. Feel the love and lightness that you feel now travel back along the entire developmental path of the fetus to conception, enfolding it with love at every step it has taken to this point. Visualize this loving enfoldment of the Spirit of the Womb extending to the future, to a safe and loving birth. Picture the child, from month one to month nine, safe in the spiritual womb of love that you are providing.

Move your hands gently in and out, in and out, as though you are expanding and contracting the bubble. Feel the energy pouring forth from your fingers and into the bubble, as you love and bless the child. Keep your hands on the edge of the bubble, wherever you feel this is. If you feel that twelve inches is too close, move your hands further away until you find the correct distance that defines the edges of your bubble. Keep that love and affirmation coming out of your fingers.

Now, gradually, move your hand further and further away, keeping the same feelings of love and appreciation flowing. Become aware of your breathing. Slowly become aware of your body, and how relaxed and refreshed you feel. Become aware of the room, and of the peace that fills it.

When you are ready, open your eyes and look around. Become aware of where you are. Look at your hand. Remember that whenever you see that hand, for the whole of today, you will remember the love and blessing that flowed through it. It will bring to your

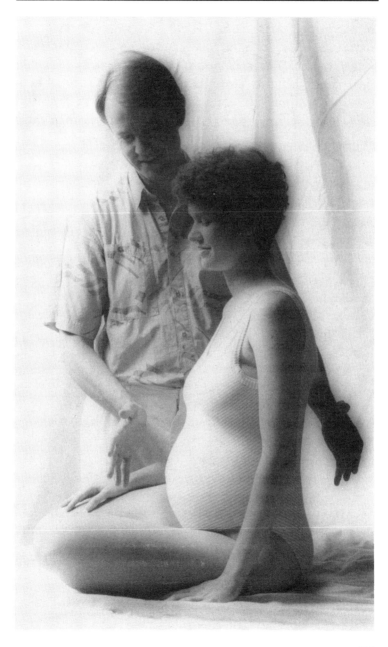

memory the Spirit of the Womb. You will remember the love you have for your baby, and the love your baby has for you. You will not forget this feeling, for you have something as close as your hand to remind you. Every time you look at your hand, you will feel love and thankfulness pouring forth from you into your child.

•••••

Sensing the Spirit of the Womb

Once you have touched the Spirit of the Womb and discovered the sanctity that accompanies it, chances are that you won't want to leave it. You will want to maintain that spirit wherever you are, whatever you are doing, for the rest of your life. For the child you are really nurturing is the child within you. Your external child is simply an icon that represents the spirit of your own inner birth. And birth is something we should all be involved with on a daily basis. We are given constant opportunities for birth; in fact, there is one every moment!

This Exercise is one you can recall throughout the day to remind you of the Spirit of the Womb. The Spirit of the Womb is something that needs to be constantly maintained. It is a space in our mind and heart that needs the constant nurture of peace and stability. As we develop that space within ourselves, we become acutely conscious of the importance of that space in the development of our child.

The incoming soul can make enormous progress if it is consciously aided by parents intent upon providing it the vibratory space in which to do its work. And our world is ready for the impact of facilitated souls. By becoming aware of the Spirit of the Womb, we give our whole planet what it requires most.

Chapter

4

Sensing the Spirit of the Fetus: The Incarnation and The Vehicle

Inner and Outer Dimensions

Just as individuals differ widely in their physical characteristics, emotional habits and mental patterning – the outer levels of being, there are similar differences in the spiritual character of each person – the inner levels of being. You are the person with whose outer levels you are most familiar. You are also very familiar with the outer levels of your partner, and if you have sought to understand the nature of your relationship on the inner levels, you have probably formed a sense of the spiritual identity of your partner as well.

By having a baby, you are inviting a third set of inner and outer characteristics into the equation. You become a triad, which creates a very different configuration of spiritual energy than two people do.

The totality of the human being is composed of the outer levels of being, with which we are reasonably familiar, and the inner levels. The outer levels are the body, mind and heart. In the world as we know it, outer bodies grow and become full-sized, so there is some development at the physical level. We also develop our minds, to some degree. This amount is only a fraction of our mind's potential, and a well-developed mind often hinders the expression of spirit.

Then we have the heart, or emotional range, which in the present dispensation usually stays miniscule. We are educated to think in terms of broad emotions such as love and hate, which is like knowing two notes out of the keyboard of a piano. If our knowledge of the emotional realm is limited to this brief repertoire of emotional experience, we are never going to make beautiful music. With hundreds of thousands of notes available, no two people need ever sound the same note twice if they are attuned to the delicate gradations of music that are possible.

When these outer capacities of body, mind and heart (the vehicle) are under the control of our spiritual or inner nature (the incarnate one), they can be used to express spirit, and manifest spirit. That is the reason we have these facilities. But when they usurp control for themselves, they are unavailable for the expression of life's energy.

In the process of birth, spirit draws together a physical form, with its mental and emotional components, in order to incarnate on earth. Each discarnate soul, in preparing to come to this plane, sets up for itself the combination of circumstances most suited to the lessons it has decided to learn and the purposes it has chosen to fulfill in the great creative scheme of things.

So there is this transcendent aspect of each person, this divine spirit, that has manifested the outer form for its use. The outer form is the vehicle for the incarnation. It is rather like a car which the driver has put together to get him from point A to point B. The soul is the driver; the body/mind/heart is the car. When this outer form of body/mind/heart is responsive to the driver, the whole combination moves from point A to point B with the least amount of fuss.

When, however, the chassis decides it wants to go one way, the engine decides it wants to go another, and the passenger compartment a third, and none of them wants to fulfill the directives of the driver, what do you have? Answer: the world as we see it today, out of the control of spirit.

This condition in the individual, with body, mind and heart pulling after their own purposes rather than the spiritual tasks for which they gathered in the first place, is akin to schizophrenia. The incarnational vehicle must be responsive to spirit in order to move with the creative flow. Out of control cars tend to get pretty dented and bashed about, which is precisely what happens to the *human* divorced from *being*. It is the *being* aspect of human beings which makes us fully ourselves.

Education for Seven Dimensional Life

A child who is nurtured on the inner levels of spirit has an immense advantage over those who aren't. If we are not taught to honor spirit when we are children, we may teach ourselves later, but the process is apt to be full of collisions and traumas. If, on the other hand, children are raised under the dominion of spirit, the chances of their incarnational vehicles being under the control of the soul is much greater.

You will not become acquainted with the outer levels of the child until the child is born, and later. You will find out about your child's body, mind and emotional realm as these aspects develop. Underlying the outer levels are the inner levels, and these you can sense long before the physical form of the child is visible. Things of the outer are discerned using the outer capacities, while things of the spirit are spiritually discerned. Using your spiritual discernment, you can be aware of the spiritual characteristics of the soul that has chosen to incarnate in the body of your child long before birth.

It may even be appropriate in some instances to come into contact with the pre-incarnate soul even before conception. A woman may have an undefined sense, long before she meets a mate, that she is destined to bring a soul into the world that will fulfill some great purpose. She may be able to form a kinship with that soul years before the physical mechanisms are in place for that soul to incarnate.

One woman reported strongly sensing the essence of the angel destined to incarnate through her body four years before conception. Another lady developed an intimate communion with the spirit of her child two years before conceiving, learning and drawing lessons from the experience which provided her with insight about her other relationships. This kind of first contact is analogous to conception on the spiritual level.

Once there is a certainty of physical-level conception, however, it is appropriate for new parents who have awakened to their full nature as spirit-beings to become conscious of, and welcome in, the spirit-being that will inhabit the body of their child. This spirit is coming to earth for a particular purpose, or set of purposes. It is not going through all the inconvenience of potty training, pimples and traffic jams just for the fun of it all!

Some are reluctant to incarnate at all, knowing the challenges they will face on the earth plane and the agonies their outer identity will go through before it discovers the being within. There is always the chance too that these problems will so distract the incarnational facilities that they will not awaken to the presence of the soul within, or do so only to a very limited level. Then the whole incarnation will have been a waste, from a practical standpoint.

The Source of Education

Parents who are conscious of these factors can make a vast difference. They can smooth the path of the incarnating soul by giving the outer form the correct conditioning, predisposing the outer form to awaken easily to the presence of the soul within. Parents unconscious of their responsibility can so load the outer form with distractions and distortions that the awakening process takes longer and is much more painful than necessary.

This is where spiritual-level sensing is so vital. Parents cannot learn what their child will require by reading child psychology textbooks Dr. Spock is no substitute for spirit-filled parenting; Dr. Ruth is no substitute for spirit-filled relationships! Textbooks speak in generalities, in principles which perhaps are typical of most children.

Your child may have *completely* different requirements. Trust spirit; trust your inner knowing; get in touch with what your child is saying to you from the womb. It does not hurt to read and to consult people. This can be very useful. The creative process often picks up bits and pieces of knowledge from our conscious mind in order to tell us something. If the knowledge is there, it can be made use of.

But the knowledge stored in the mind or in books or in other people's minds, even those of "experts," should not dictate what we do. Spirit should dictate. Educated people are no better at sensing spirit than those whose outer minds are less cultivated. Brilliance of mind is no advantage. Truly brilliant people are those who have yielded to spirit, whose behavior is controlled by the urges of creation. They have let the dominion of spirit infuse the outer mind and emotions; control has shifted from the outer form of body/mind/heart to the Being of Truth within.

If spiritual education has taken place, all other education will fall into line when and if required. If spiritual education has not taken place, no amount of worldly education will suffice. More training may even form additional layers of sophistication which distance a person from the urges of spirit. Our babies do not require us to be Ph.D.'s. They DO require us to be one with the inner truth of who we are. From this vantage point, we can do far more to ease their passage into the world than any amount of outer-mind knowing.

This inner knowing is like any other human capacity. in that it grows as we develop it. Just as our muscles grow as they are used, our sensitivity to spirit grows as we employ it. In developing any of our capacities, inner or outer, the word is: "Use It or Lose It!" Physical muscles may be of help in performing physical tasks. They are no use in performing spiritual tasks.

Tuning In

As we begin to tune in to a baby, our perceptions may be faint and indistinct at first, but will become more precise with use. We aren't given much scope for developing these sensitivities as we grow up, so we tend to grow up without them. The advent of a new baby is a great opportunity to begin to develop our faculties of spiritual perception. And this sensitivity will allow our baby to communicate its needs to us.

One mother was a vegetarian, and her outer mind was convinced that this was the best possible form of nutrition. Imagine her horror when, channeling the spirit of her fetus, the child demanded that during gestation she eat meat! Lots of it! And RED meat! Had she remained unaware of what the spirit required for the development of the physical form of the baby, she would have been unable to co-operate.

The following Exercise may be used to contact the spirit of the fetus. Before you begin, put yourself in a physical environment that is still and free of distractions. A darkened room may be helpful. Play, at very low volume, some soothing music. You can have a friend or your partner read you the Exercise, or you can tape it and play it back. Have some paper handy so that you can write down your experiences once you are done.

45

•••••

First Exercise

Close your eyes. Breathe out, exhaling all the old, stale air from your lungs. Relax, and allow pure, clean, fresh air to be drawn back in. Breathe out and in in this manner several times. With each outbreath, feel the tension leave your body. As you breathe in, feel fresh air streaming over your brain and mind, washing out all mental preoccupations. Let all your concerns, your worries, fade into the background. Let the cool, white incoming air soothe your frustrations, smoothing over the rough patches in your life.

Visualize your body as being filled with green energy. This green energy is all the stored tensions that have been retained in your muscles and organs. See how this energy fills all of your limbs. Start at your feet. On each outbreath, feel the energy flowing out of your feet with the breath. Take as many outbreaths as required to clear out this green fluid from every nook and cranny of your feet.

Then go up your calves, thighs, pelvis, and work your way up. When you have completely cleared your shoulders of this fluid green energy, and each part of your body feels completely limp, see the energy that fills your head. Start at the back of your skull, and begin to expel it with each breath. Keep going till even the smallest cavities in your head have been emptied of the green energy, and no tension or tightness remain.

Finally, empty your neck and mouth of the fluid, and feel how completely relaxed your body has become.

Now let your attention review each part of your body again, to see if there are still any remaining pockets of the tension-energy. Find the subtle places where tension is still lingering, and allow it to flow easily out of you on the current of your breath.

You are now an empty form, limp and flaccid. Behind you, though, you can sense the presence of another being. This other being is a beautiful, shining presence. It is nothing but love for you. Its presence enfolds you, and you melt into it. In the bubble of its presence, you know that you are perfectly safe. In its presence you are at home. It welcomes you into itself, and your heart can rest in the knowledge that you have come home. You are free, safe and secure. You feel an upsurge of thankfulness that you have contacted this being, who is your true self, at last. Your years of wandering are over, and you can rest in the peace of having found yourself.

Feel how perfect this being is, how beautiful. Feel how there is nothing in the bubble of energy that is this being that could possibly threaten you, disturb you or upset you. It is fully you. It is truly you. Look and see the appearance of this being that is your true self. Notice the gorgeous colors, the perfect shapes. Spend as much time as you like just appreciating the wonder of this being. Notice details about its form, and how it flows. Merge every part of yourself with it in ecstatic union.

Now take time to look around you, around you two-who-have-merged-into-one. Notice that there is another such being of light. It is the true being of the one who is closest to you, of your partner in love. Notice how perfect the essence of your partner is. See your partner coming slowly towards you, till your light-forms are close to each other.

Notice those things that were special to you the first time you saw your partner. Notice how there are also those things in your partner which are not part of their true being; bits of unnecessary baggage they are carrying around, which are a hindrance. Reach out and bless your partner. Reach out your hands of healing and touch the parts of them that have not been integrated into their true being. Feel yourself loving them – all of them – the light and the dark places alike. Feel your power to embrace your partner, and the strength and affirmation your partner derives from your embrace. Feel how the sum of your power together is greater than either of you have as individuals. Sense your light shining more brightly as you come together: an increase of radiance. Thank the spirit of your partner for coming to be with you.

Now the two of you turn your attention outward, to become aware of another spirit. You notice that this spirit is different from the two of you. Its shining bubble of spirit is as large and as complex as your own. But the portion that represents the physical body is very small and unformed as yet. It is a spiritual giant in a tiny physical form. It is some distance away from you, and you beckon it closer. It moves toward you slowly. Do not try to pull it towards you any closer than it wishes to come. Let it find the distance between you which it is comfortable for it. It can stay at this distance while you become familiar with each other.

Notice the details of it. What colors are part of it? In what patterns do they move? What other characteristics does it have? Is it speaking to you? If so, what does it say? If it does not speak, do not try and force it. Just be there, fully present. Ask it what you can do for it in order to prepare for its incarnation. It may not respond with anything at all, or it may have a lengthy list of suggestions. Note carefully anything it tries to communicate, but do not pressure it to communicate.

Form your bubble of energy to a point that faces your fetus. Now make the point lengthen, like a strand of straight rope that goes out from you towards the spirit of the fetus. See this bright channel of energy reach your fetus, and join with its bubble of energy. Now feel energy flowing from you to the fetus. Let it feel your love and concern, your assurance that you want only what is best. Feel its energy flowing back along the path towards you. Receive that energy. Embrace it, make it one with you. Feel yourself enriched by this gift of light from another.

Then let the encounter draw to a close. As you are preparing to part, let the fetus decide if it wants to maintain the energy link, or to let it go for now, till the next time. If it wants to go, gently release your energy strand and let it blend back into you.

Thank the spirit of the fetus for coming to be with you, and sense it fade into the distance. Thank your partner for blending with you in this experience. Give your partner a final embrace, and allow them to fade away too. Become aware of how you are breathing; in and out, in and out, in and out. Feel your light form filling your physical form. Feel every part of your body filled with this radiant light. Appreciate each part of your physical body. When you are ready, open your *eyes. Write down what you have just seen and felt. Write as many specifics as possible.*

•••••

The First Exercise in this chapter is a general introduction to the spirit of the baby, in which we just let the nature of the contact be whatever it will be. This Exercise can be done several times, until you feel really comfortable being with the spirit of the child.

The purpose of the Second Exercise is to bring the level of communication from the general level to the specific. Once a pattern of communion is firmly established between the adults and the child, more specific information can be exchanged. It is rather like any human encounter; we need to feel comfortable in the presence of another human being before we begin to tell them our deepest secrets. We don't jump to deeper levels until we feel comfortable together. The First Exercise is designed to set the stage in this way.

Use the First Exercise till this stage of familiarity is reached, then switch over to the Second Exercise. Before beginning, set up the room so you are comfortable, as you did before. Keep pen and paper handy, so that you can write down your observations at the end.

•••••

Second Exercise

Close your eyes. Breathe out, exhaling all the old, stale air from your lungs. Relax, and allow pure, clean, fresh air to be sucked back in. Breathe out and in in this manner several times. With each outbreath, feel the tension leave your body.

As you breathe in, feel the fresh air streaming over your brain and mind, washing out all the pre-occupations in your head. Let all your concerns, your worries, fade into the background. Let the cool, white incoming air soothe your frustrations, smoothing over the rough patches in your life.

Visualize your body as being filled with green energy. This green energy is all the stored tensions that have been retained in your muscles and organs. See how this energy fills all of your limbs. Start at your feet. On each outbreath, feel the energy flowing out of your feet with the breath. Take as many outbreaths as required to clear out this green fluid from every nook and cranny of your feet.

Then go up your calves, thighs, pelvis, and work your way up. Allow the green energy to flow out of your shoulders on your breath, then clear your head and neck. Keep going till no tension or tightness remain. Feel how completely relaxed your body has become.

Now let your attention review each part of your body again, to see if there are still any remaining pockets of the tension-energy. Find the subtle places where tension still lingers and allow it to flow easily out of you on the current of your breath.

You are now an empty form, limp and flaccid. Behind you, you can sense the presence of your true being. It is a beautiful, shining presence. It is nothing but love for you. Once again its presence enfolds you, and you melt into it. In the bubble of its presence, you know that you are perfectly safe. You know that you

51

have come home. It feels wonderful to be with your light-self again. It welcomes you into itself, and you feel free, safe and secure.

Feel how perfect this true you is, how beautiful. Feel how there is nothing in the bubble of energy that is this being that could possibly threaten you, disturb you or upset you. It is fully you. It is truly you. Look and see the appearance of this being that is you. Look at the gorgeous colors, the perfect shapes.

Spend as much time as you like just appreciating the wonder of this being. Notice details about its form, and how it flows. Has it changed at all since you were with it last? Is it more distinct? Are its colors brighter? Merge every part of your outer self with it in ecstatic union.

Now take time to look around you, around you two-who-have-merged-into-one. Notice the light-presence of your partner coming towards you. See your partner coming slowly towards you, till your light-forms are close to each other. Notice how perfect your partner is. Has your partner changed at all since you saw them last?

Reach out and bless your partner. Reach out your hands of healing and touch the parts of their outer being that have not been integrated into their true being. Feel yourself loving them – all of them – light and dark places. Feel your power to embrace your partner, and the strength and affirmation your partner derives from your embrace. Feel how the sum of your power together is greater than either of you have as individuals. Sense your radiance increasing as you come together. Thank the spirit of your partner for coming to be with you.

Now the two of you turn your attention outward, to become aware of another spirit, the spirit of your baby. Its shining bubble of spirit is as large and as complex as your own. But the portion that represents the physical body is very small and unformed as yet. It is a spiritual giant and a physical pygmy. It is some distance away from you, and you beckon it closer. It moves toward you. Do not try to pull it towards you any closer than it wishes to come. Let it find the distance between you which it is comfortable for it. Is this distance different from the previous time you saw it?

Just be there, fully present. Note the details. Can you see any details you could not see before?

Form your bubble of energy to a point that faces your fetus. Now make the point lengthen, into a strand of energy that goes out from you towards the spirit of the fetus. See this bright channel of energy reach your fetus, and join with its bubble of energy. Now feel energy flowing from you to the fetus. Let it feel your love and concern, your assurance that you want only what is best. Feel its energy flowing back along the path towards you. Receive that energy. Embrace it, make it one with you. Feel yourself enriched by this gift of light from another.

Ask the spirit of the fetus what it needs from you. Ask it specific questions, and give it time to reply. If it does not reply after a little while, move on the the next question. Ask it:

What do I and my partner need to eat that will serve the needs of your growing body?
What sort of physical environment does my body need in order to nurture yours?

What sort of mental environment must I maintain in order to nurture yours?

What sort of emotional climate do I need to maintain in order to nurture yours?

What physical habits do I have that obstruct your growth and function?

What mental habits do I have that obstruct your growth and function?

What emotional habits do I have that obstruct your growth and function?

What habits in my relationship with my partner do I have that obstruct your coming into your own?

What sorts of people would you like around you while you are an infant, and cannot speak to me?

What sorts of people would you like around you when you are a child?

What physical place would best serve your growth?

What is your primary purpose in coming to Earth?

What are some of your secondary purposes?

How can I help you with those?

What are some of my purposes?

How can you help me with these?

What is your name?

Do you have any closely related souls incarnating around this same time?

Are there any books you would like me to read?

Are there any people you would like me to talk to?

What style of birthing would you most prefer?

Who would you like as a (midwife, nurse, doctor)?

Which friends and relatives, if any, would you like at the birth?

How can I minimize stress for you after birth?

How can I minimize stress for myself after your birth?

How can I minimize stress for my partner after your birth?

What color room would you like as a baby?

What else should I know before your birth?

What is the most important thing you would like me to remember after your birth?

What else would you like to tell me?

Let the encounter draw to a close. As you are preparing to part, let the fetus decide if it wants to maintain the energy link, or to let it go for now, till the next time. If it wants to go, gently release your energy strand and let it blend back into you.

Thank the spirit of the fetus for coming to be with you, and sense it fade into the distance. Thank your partner for blending with you in this experience. Give your partner a final embrace, and allow them to fade away too.

Become aware of how you are breathing: in and out, in and out, in and out. Feel your light form filling your physical form. Feel every part of your body filled with this radiant light. Feel and appreciate each part of your physical body. Feel yourself affirmed and strengthened by this experience. Enjoy your new sense of connection with the fetus, and know that it will be with you all day. When you are ready, open your eyes. Write down as many specifics as possible.

•••••

Repeat this Exercise, using your own list of questions. You may turn back to the Exercise from time to time for answers, as more specific situations arise in your life. As your relationship with the spirit of the fetus grows, you may find yourself being able to ask it more and more specific questions.

You Are In Control

Don't hesitate to check the information it gives you with other sources. If your partner is doing these Exercises with you, their experience is a valuable check on your own.

In evaluating the information you get from these sessions, use your discretion. If you feel your fetus is demanding that you drink three glasses of undiluted sulfuric acid a day, check on the effects of sulfuric acid on the human body before you do so!

These Exercises are *not* a substitute for our minds, and the intuition and sensing we feel from other sources. As multifaceted beings, we must honor the wisdom of *all* aspects of ourselves. These Exercises may put us in touch with one aspect. But to go overboard in one aspect and ignore the others misses the fulness of ourselves.

Don't be uncritical of the information you receive in your meditation times. *You* **are the one who is in control of the process.** You are not abandoning responsibility to a being who is guiding you from another plane.

But once you accept your own spiritual identity, you are in position to receive information on that level from the spiritual identity of your fetus, and establish a link long before birth. This information can help you prepare for the event.

Chapter

5

Radiance Exercises

Bio-Energy Fields

Around each person is an invisible field of energy referred to by Eastern mystics as the aura; by Russian medical researchers as the bioplasmic field (bio=life; plasm=substance); by physicists as an electromagnetic field. It extends two to five feet from the physical body in more or less an egg shape from head to foot.

The colors in the field differ from person to person, depending on the individual's characteristics. A person's field will change continuously, reflecting the general state of health, specific diseases, the emotional state, whether one is awake or asleep, etc.

When two people are together, their auras interact even when no physical contact takes place. Those who are more sensitive to auric qualities can consciously

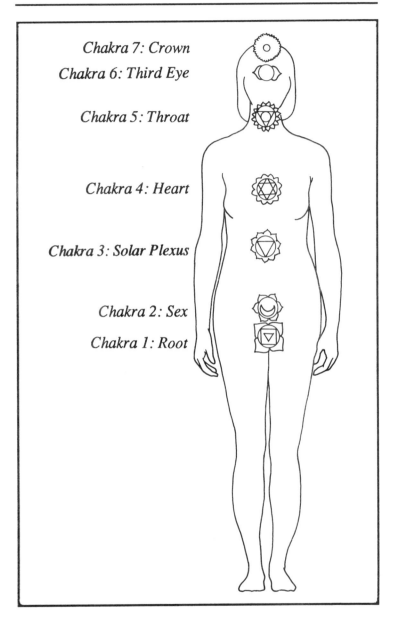

Chakra 7: Crown
Chakra 6: Third Eye

Chakra 5: Throat

Chakra 4: Heart

Chakra 3: Solar Plexus

Chakra 2: Sex
Chakra 1: Root

Chakras

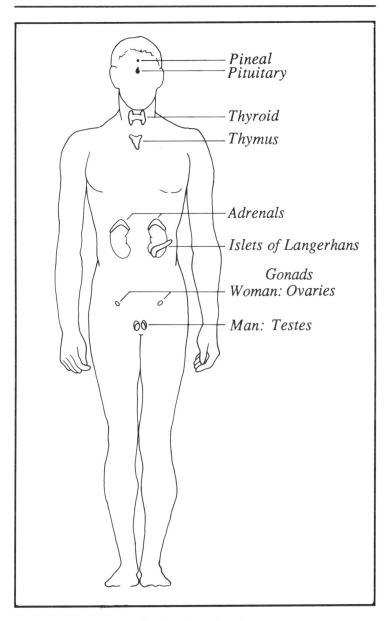

Endocrine glands

pick up information from the auras of others. Part of intuition is the ability to read the auric signals we are giving out all the time about our intentions, our general state and our specific qualities.

Within this field of invisible energy that penetrates the physical body of each person, there are specific focus points for different kinds of energy. These are sometimes referred to as the chakras. Each chakra corresponds to a particular quality. There are seven chakras.

The Endocrine System

On the physical level, the manifestation of these invisible bioenergetic points is the endocrine system. There are seven endocrine glands. They are also referred to as the ductless glands, because, unlike sebaceous glands, salivary glands, etc., their secretions do not flow through ducts to other parts of the body. The secretions of the endocrine glands pass directly into the bloodstream, and thus have an immediate effect on the entire body. The best known example is that of the adrenal glands. When they are stimulated into the secretion of adrenaline, the "fight or flight" mechanism readies the whole body in seconds to respond to the exigencies of an emergency situation.

Sensing the Inner Levels

Because of this correlation between the bio-energetic and physical systems, many therapeutic effects can be obtained by attending to the bioenergetic factors, without recourse to physical levels. You don't need to touch the body, in other words, to have effects on the body. The invisible levels of wellness virtually always underlie physical wellness.

With practice, it is possible to develop our awareness of these invisible levels of being. As we raise our sensitivity to this whole field of function, our invisible senses become more and more acute, and we see more of what is happening in these areas. We rely less on what we can see, smell, hear, touch and taste and more on what we "sense without senses" to construct our picture of the world and of other people.

Utilizing this area of perception, we can interact with the unborn child, connecting in a powerful, radiant way on a spiritual level. The Exercise below can be done with a child *in utero,* or a newborn, or an older child. It is easier if the child is asleep.

Specific Pattern – Mother only

General Pattern – Father only

•••••

Exercise One

Make yourself comfortable in a quiet room that is not too bright. Become aware of your breathing. Breathe slowly in and out, allowing all the concerns of the day to exit on your outbreaths. Feel your mind becoming quiet as you focus on your breath. Feel your heart becoming still, as all the things that have disturbed it flow out of your body on your breath. Keep focusing on your breathing, in and out, until your body, mind and heart are all perfectly still.

Visualize a beam of light coming down from above to rest on your head. This beam is white, shining, pure, and bathes you with a gentle radiance. Imagine the source of the light. The light is coming from the Lord of light, the Supreme Being of love, the One who has ultimate responsibility for the co-ordination of this planet. Whatever your highest vision of Godhead is, imagine the light proceeding from this One to touch the top of your head. Feel your responsiveness to this infinite sea of love. Your thankfulness ascends back up the light beam.

Now visualize the beam of light flowing over your body and down your arms to your hands. As it flows over your hands, hold your hands in such a way as to focus this energy, as though you were pointing it, using all four fingers and your thumb.

See the shining essence of your partner coming towards you. Direct the stream of energy you create with your hands toward the energy field of your partner. As the energy touches them, the colors and intensity of their energy field intensify. Keep your energy beam tightly focused, using your fingers as a pointer. As you bathe them in this radiance, feel how they respond to your invisible touch.

Now open your hands so that the energy is more diffused. Hold them about a foot to eighteen inches away from the baby. Gently allow this diffused energy to make contact with the baby's energy field. Keep a stable radiance coming from your hands, and feel the intensification of your own field and that of the baby.

Allow the intensity of the love radiance pouring from your hands to increase. Let the pressure build, but to a point at which it is still comfortable to the child. Allow the current coming from you to increase, and an intensified response to reciprocate from the child.

Hold this current of love steady. Keep in mind that you are not the originator of this stream of love, but the transmitter. Remain totally responsive to the One above whose energy you are focusing. Keep your mind centered in the beam of love coming to you from above.

You may feel certain patterns in the energy field of the baby shift. Don't try too hard to figure out what they are, for this will take your mind off of its connection to the One above. Whatever you feel happening, <u>stay connected upwards</u>. Do not let your mind stray. Keep your response flowing upward towards the Supreme One even as the light streams from your hands to the baby.

After a certain amount of time, you may feel that the pattern of radiance is complete. When this occurs, allow the intensity of the energy coming from your hands to taper off gently. Move your hands further from the child. Move slowly, being careful to keep the connection with the baby.

Turn your hands so that the palms point upward. Let your thanks flow upward to God for the privilege of transmitting and sharing His energy.

When you have given thanks, turn your palms inward and place your hands on your heart. Feel how *still your heart and mind are, and how full. Remember this feeling whenever you see your hand today. Remember it throughout the whole day, especially when you are distracted, or when events come up to pull your emotions off center.*

Feel your breathing once more. Experience the air flowing gently in and out. Feel how refreshed and new you feel. Give thanks for this experience, and open your eyes when you are ready.

•••••

The Vital Importance of Maintaining Upward Orientation

During this Exercise it is important to keep your own patterns of consciousness out of the picture. The more intense the experience, the more likely that your mind and heart will become stirred up. Strong spiritual experiences may jar loose various excited thought patterns. If you take your attention away from the moment in order to explore some attractive thought that pops up out of the subconscious, you will remove yourself from the present moment and what is really happening.

The purpose of this Exercise is not to generate fodder for the mind. **You are working with extremely sensitive and delicate areas of your baby's well-being. It is CRUCIAL to remain <u>centered</u>** while engaging in this type of work. This is done by remaining focused on your connection with the One above, and **not allowing your attention to be distracted from this One by what is happening around you OR WITHIN YOU.** The life stream must be held steady, by a mind and heart that are totally focused on channeling spirit from above.

If you discover you do not have the training yet to do this, contact someone at one of the Attunement Centers listed in the back of this book in the Resources section. In these places you will find people with many years of experience in maintaining this upward connection as the life stream is focused. The guidance of an experienced person is highly recommended during this delicate and lovely process of connecting parents and child.

Forming Radiant Habits

If you are doing this with a young child, you may observe the child's body moving during the course of the Exercise. You may notice rapid eye movements, or limb movements, or settling in and getting comfortable, or even discomfort.

Once you are practiced in the art of focusing this divine radiance, you will discover that you begin to do it instinctively. You no longer react to crises by becoming bent out of shape. Instead, you regard crises as opportunities to send out this spiritual radiance to the individuals involved, or to your own disturbed mind and heart. You instinctively adopt a radiant stance whenever the road gets rocky. Spirit becomes your primary resource for dealing with any situation.

In subsequent chapters we will begin to consider the factors involved in directing the flow of the life current into each of the seven primary physical contact points. You will use the same Exercise for each one, but a different Meditation. The **Exercise** puts you in touch with all the specific contact points in the child's body into which you can direct the radiance of love. The **Radiance Meditation** is a conscious invocation of the spirit associated with that physical point.

Spirit Creates Form

Each endocrine gland has a corresponding spirit. The spirit is the divine quality with which that part of the body is associated. When we direct radiance to a particular part of the body, we are not primarily working with the physical organ. We are not primarily interested in effecting change on the physical level.

Spirit underlies form. As we do our appropriate work on the spiritual level, the physical levels of things fall into place. There is no need for us to try and manipulate physical form to try and make it right. As the spirit is right, the form will follow. So although we use the endocrine glands as contact points, we are not doing the Exercise for the benefit of the glands. We are doing it for the benefit of the whole, and wholeness is found in spirit.

Spirit is not an undifferentiated mass, as you will know from the above Exercise. It has particular characteristics. Around these spiritual vortices, physical form takes shape. The purpose of the Exercises is to promote an effective connection between spirit and form.

Disease results from a blockage of the connection between spirit and form. The goal of these Exercises is not to effect any particular change in form. It is to allow a free flow of spirit to form, with the understanding that when it is allowed free access, spirit will make whatever changes are required in form.

There are certain spiritual poles around which physical matter is organized. Each primary radiation point in the physical body, each endocrine gland, has a particular spirit with which it is associated. The following chart lists these correlations.

GLAND:	SPIRIT:
Pineal	Love
Pituitary	Womb
Thyroid	Life
Thymus	Purity
Islets of Langerhans	Blessing
Adrenals	Purpose
Gonads	Earth

As we move though each one, you will become sensitive to each spirit, and the effect that spirit (and the absence of it) has on physical form. You will nurture each of these aspects in the child, and encourage an optimal transfer of energy between the spirit of the child and the form.

Methods

The following Exercise will familiarize you with these contact points in the baby. You can do this Exercise with a child *in utero,* after birth, at any age (preferably while the child is asleep – for reasons which are obvious to anyone with young children!), or with your partner as the subject.

If both partners wish to participate in doing this

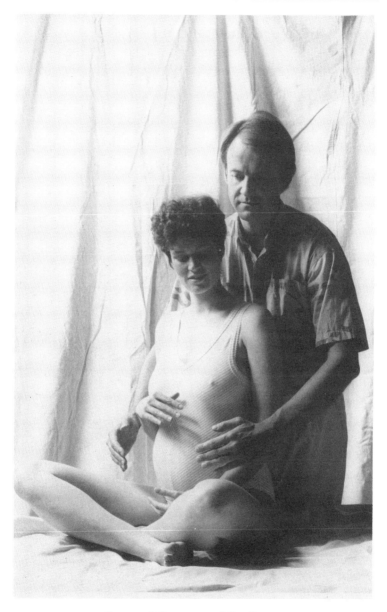

General Pattern of Radiance

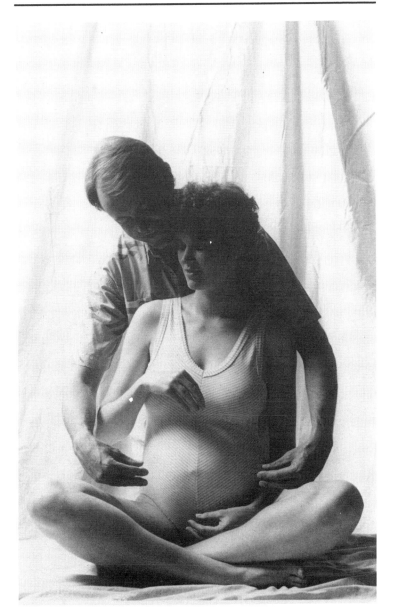

Specific Pattern of Radiance

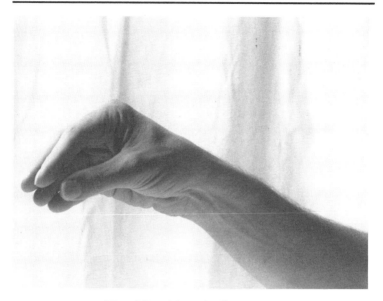

Hand Position A: Strong Focus

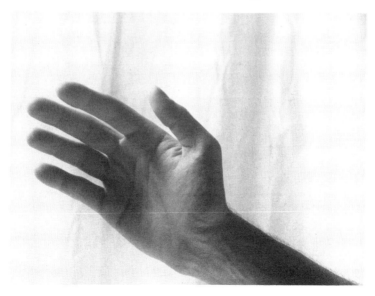

Hand Position B: Soft Focus

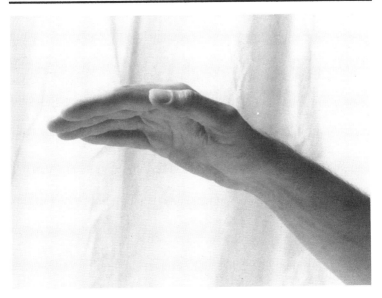

Hand Position B: Soft Focus

Case	Hand Position:	Exercise:
Both Parents Child *in Utero*	Mother: A and Father: B or Mother: B and Father: A	Mother: 2 and Father: 1 or Mother: 1 and Father: 2
Both Parents, Sleeping Child	One: A the other: B	A parent does 2 B parent does 1
One Parent, Sleeping Child	A B	2 1
Mother Only, Child in Utero	A B	2 1
Father Only, Child in Utero	A B	2 1

with the child as the subject, one partner should do the above Exercise, holding a *general* pattern of radiation, while the other does the Exercise below, which involves a *specific* pattern (See photographs on pages 69 and 70). It is also possible for one parent to offer radiation to the child using the contact points on the other parent. In other words, one parent does it with the other as subject, always bearing the child in mind.

For a mother doing this Exercise alone, with her child *in utero* as the subject, hand positions A and B may also be used. See the chart and illustrations below for details.

Before you begin Exercise Two, put yourself in a physical environment that is still, and free of distractions. A darkened room may be helpful, with just a little light present. Play, at very low volume, some soothing music. You can have a friend or your partner read you the Meditation, or you can tape it and play the tape back. If you have the meditation tape also entitled Communing with the Spirit of Your Unborn Child, you can use that.

If two partners are each doing one of the two Exercises, both should use the first ten paragraphs of Exercise Two. After that, one continues with Exercise two while the other picks up at paragraph five of Exercise One. Review the endocrine diagram at the beginning of this chapter before commencing this Exercise.

•••••

Exercise Two

Close your eyes. Breathe out, exhaling all the old, stale air from your lungs. Relax, and allow pure, clean, fresh air to be sucked back in. Breathe out and in in this manner several times. With each outbreath, feel the tension leave your body. As you breathe in, feel the fresh air streaming over your brain and mind, washing out all the thoughts in your head. Let all your concerns, your worries, fade into the background. Let the cool, white incoming air soothe your frustrations, smoothing over the rough patches in your life.

Visualize your body as being filled with green energy. This green energy is all the stored tensions that have been retained in your muscles and organs. Picture this energy filling all of your limbs. Start at your feet. On each outbreath, feel the energy flowing out of your feet with the breath. Take as many outbreaths as required to clear out this green fluid from every nook and cranny of your feet.

Then go up your calves, thighs, pelvis, and work your way up. Spend enough time on each place to allow all the green tension energy to flow out of you completely. When you have completely cleared your shoulders of this fluid green energy, and each part of your body feels completely limp, see the energy that fills your head. Start at the back of your skull, and begin to expel it with each breath. Keep going till even the smallest cavities in your head have been emptied of the green energy, and no tension or tightness remain.

Finally, empty your neck and mouth of the fluid,

and feel how completely relaxed your body has become.

Now let your attention review each part of your body again, to see if there are still any remaining pockets of the tension-energy. Find the subtle places where tension is still lingering, and allow it to flow easily out of you on the current of your breath.

You are now an empty form, limp and flaccid. Behind you, though, you can sense the presence of another being. This other being is a beautiful, shining presence. It is nothing but love for you. Its presence enfolds you, and you melt into it. In the bubble of its presence, you know that you are perfectly safe. In its presence you are at home. It welcomes you into itself, and your heart can rest in the knowledge that you have come home. You are free, safe and secure. You feel an upsurge of thankfulness that you have contacted this being, who is your true self, once again.

Feel how perfect this being is, how beautiful. Feel how there is nothing in the bubble of energy that is this being that could possibly threaten you, disturb you or upset you. It is fully you. It is truly you. Look and see the appearance of this being that is you. Look at the gorgeous colors, the perfect shapes. Spend as much time as you would like just appreciating the wonder of this being. Notice details about its form, and how it flows. Merge every part of yourself with it in ecstatic union.

Visualize a beam of light coming down from above to rest on your head. This beam is white, shining, pure, and bathes you with a gentle radiance. Imagine the source of the light. The light is coming from the Lord of light, the supreme being of love, the One who has ultimate responsibility for the coordination of this world. Whatever your highest vision of godhead is, imagine the light proceeding from this One to touch the top of your head. Feel your responsiveness to this infinite sea of love. Feel your thankfulness ascending back up the light beam.

Now visualize the beam of light flowing over your body and down your arms to your hands. As it flows over your hands, hold your hands in such a way as to focus this energy, as though you were pointing it, using all four fingers and your thumb (Hand Position A). Direct the stream of energy you create in this way towards the energy field of your child. As the energy touches the child, the colors and intensity of their energy field intensify. Keep your energy beam tightly focused using your fingers as a pointer. As you bathe them in this radiance, feel how they respond to your invisible touch.

Now open your hands so that the energy is more diffused (Hand Position B). Hold them about a foot to eighteen inches away from the baby. Keep a stable radiance coming from your hands, and feel the intensification of your own field and that of the baby. Notice the details of it. What colors are part of it? In what patterns do they move? What other characteristics does it have? Has it changed since you sensed it last?

Once you have felt the general energy field of the baby, and directed your radiance towards it using your flat hands, point your fingers to focus the energy more precisely. (Hand Position A). From a general glow around your hands, the energy becomes a focused beam.

Direct this beam to a point at the junction of the

child's head and torso. The head represents the heavenly place of control, and the torso represents the earthly place of response. As you are doing this, hold a strong image of your child always responding to the creative currents that come from Heaven in every moment. Feel any blockages that impede this current dissolving, so that the current of heavenly intent flows freely from Heaven, the realm of control, into the earth, the realm of response. Imagine your child always balanced at this crossover point, joining Heaven and earth in the divine union of creative energies. (Radiance Meditation One).

Once you sense that this pattern of right action is established in the fetus, you will feel that this point of radiance is complete and it is time to move on.

Move your hands, focusing them on a point in the center of the top of the child's head. Become aware of the connection point on the top of your own head with the silver cord coming down from Heaven. Feel the energy pouring from your hands connecting with that same point on the top of the child's head. Picture the silver cord that comes from the top of the child's head going up into Heaven. As the energy radiates from your hands, see that heavenly connection strengthening. See the child's cord pulsating with the energy coming down from above. Feel the love that is pouring in to the child from this connection with spirit (Radiance Meditation Two).

Spend a few minutes just rejoicing in this flow. Enjoy it. Then, when the flow is steady, unwavering, firmly established, move on to the next contact point.

The next contact point is just below the first, moving from the top of the child's head down the body. It is the pituitary gland. It represents the Spirit of the Womb. It is so close to the pineal that you hardly have to move your hands to touch it. Cradle the Spirit of the Womb in your hands. Feel this spirit grow strong as you pour your spirit out upon it. Feel the energy moving though your hands to energize this part of the child. As the radiant current intensifies, feel your own pituitary gland start to glow. The Spirit of the Womb is a symbol of the place where Truth dwells. Truth is the control point for the rest of the body. As you touch this gland you extend your radiant influence to all the other glands and systems (Radiance Meditation Three).

Spend a few minutes just rejoicing in this contact. Then, when the contact is steady, unwavering, firmly established, gently move on to the next contact point.

The thyroid gland represents the Spirit of Life. As you move your hand down to make connection with this spirit, imagine your child glowing with life. Imagine the child's whole experience to be vibrant, rich, confident. Become aware of your breathing once again. Breathe the breath of life into the child's third chakra. With each breath you let out, visualize breathing out a gentle, pale blue fluid into your child's throat. Picture this blue fluid bestowing on your child a full life, a wonderful life (Radiance Meditation Four).

When you have a steady pattern of connection with the thyroid, move on to the next point.

The thymus gland represents the Spirit of Purification. As you move your hand down to make contact with this point, see your child being cleansed of all the impurities that will go through them. See them easily processing all the negative energy that they receive. *It passes easily through their system, not affecting them. Any poison that they ingest, physically, emotionally or mentally, passes easily through them, as their filtration system has no trouble in handling it. As they pass through the world on their journey, they are able to purify the earth by their passage* (Radiance Meditation Five).

When you sense that the child's purification system is working properly, enjoy the perfection of it for a few moments, then go on to the next contact point.

The Islets of Langerhans represent the Spirit of Blessing. See your child blessing people as a pattern in their life. See the life of your child being a blessing to God. Imagine your child as a radiant being whose every step through the earth brings blessing to all they touch. See God being pleased with the child.

Imagine your child's hand touching the hands of all the people they will ever meet, and those hands being blessed by the touch of this blessed hand. Envision your child being ingenious in finding ways to bless people that no one else can touch. See your child's capacity to bless growing strong as you radiate energy to it from your hands (Radiance Meditation Six).

When the pattern of blessing is strong and stable in your child, move your hands down to the next contact point.

The Spirit of Purpose is represented in the human body by the adrenal glands. See your child as having singleness of purpose. This child's single purpose will be to serve God. Don't try and place any strong specific image on what this might mean. The child will find its own way of serving God. But the spirit of single-

ness of purpose means that the child will always have its eyes fixed on the most important thing in life: the connection upwards to God.

The child may live in the world, but it will always have its vision trained on the divine. Its eyes will be unwaveringly fixed on its divine purpose; it will remain undistracted by lesser purposes. With a fixity of purpose, it will prosper in all that it does. It will see God in everything. It will lead a magical life, full of wonder. With its purpose fixed in God, all else will fall into place. Everything else will work for this baby, if this focus of spirit is there (Radiance Meditation Seven).

Celebrate with your child, through the radiance of your hands, the Spirit of Singleness of Purpose. When you sense that this pattern of obedience is firm and unwavering in the child, move your hands downward to the next contact point.

The Gonads or sexual glands represent the Spirit of the New Earth. As you allow radiance to pour through your hands directed at this point on the baby's body, fill your mind with the Spirit of the New Earth. The New Earth is what is created when the New Heaven is in place.

When your baby's spiritual orientation is stead-fast, centered in the New Heaven, all the forms that this child requires for creation on the earth plane, the New Earth, will be there. We sense so strongly in this moment that the spirit of things underlies the form of things. This baby will be finely attuned to spirit. With this orientation, the form of things will fall into place automatically.

Picture your baby creating things effortlessly on

the earth plane because the spirit plane is the primary reality for them. They are not responsive to the earth; they are responsive to Heaven, and as a result, Heaven floods down to manifest through them into the earth. As this happens through your baby, the earth is made new. It rejoices to be renewed, remade, blessed and recreated by the presence upon it of God-centered human beings. Your baby will renew the earth, as it lives in Heaven (Radiance Meditation Eight).

Once you feel a strong connection made with the Spirit of the New Earth through the Gonads of your baby, enjoy feeling the energy of it for a few moments.

Once you are done with radiation to the gonads, move your hands back up the baby's body to the point where you started: the neck area, between head and torso. Feel the current of connection between the Spirit of Heaven and the Spirit of Earth, moving through this point on the baby's body. This current may feel measurably stronger now than when you began, or it may feel the same. Either way is fine. Celebrate for a few minutes the power of life moving down from Heaven into manifestation in the earth through the body of your child (Radiance Meditation Twelve).

Now move your hands gently upwards as though you were cradling the top of the baby's head. Let your hands move from a point of strong focus (Hand Position A) *to a point of soft focus* (Hand Position B). *Imagine you are cradling the baby's mind. Picture the thoughts that are filling their mind at this moment being full of creativity and peace.*

Visualize this child blessing everyone they come into contact with their whole life long, through the thoughts that pass through their brain. Picture their conscious mind being able to easily give articulation to the beauty that lives within them. Picture their words and thoughts moving out to thousands of people during their lifetime, bringing healing to everyone they ever think about or talk to (Radiance Meditation Nine).

Once you have spent some time surrounding the baby's head in this way, move your hands again. One hand should be on either side of the cord that connects the baby to Heaven above. Keeping your hands open, let your palms face away from the baby and towards Heaven. Give thanks for the experience you have just had. Give thanks for the miracle of being able to connect consciously with your baby.

Give this child that you have been given back to Heaven as a gift. Know that it is not your child, but Heaven's child. This child is Heaven's way of blessing the earth. This child is the mechanism by which the Spirit of Heaven may touch the Spirit of Earth. Present the child as a living offering to Heaven.

Give thanks for the privilege you have just had of conducting the Spirits of Heaven down into the child, through the medium of your own capacities of heart, mind, body and spirit. Feel how refreshed these capacities are by their channeling of the divine into human form. Become aware of how you are breathing; in and out, in and out, in and out. Feel your light form filling your physical form. Feel every part of your body filled with this radiant light. Feel and appreciate each part of your physical body. When you are ready, open your eyes.

•••••

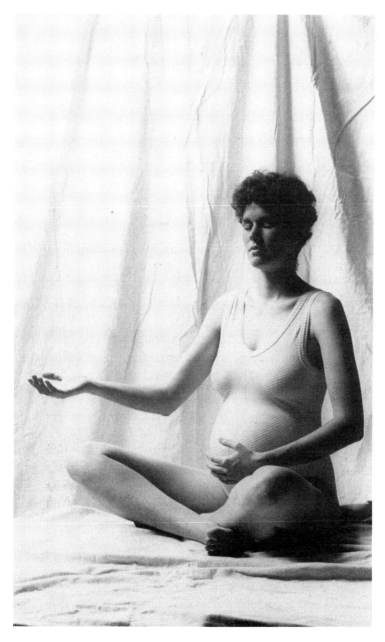

Variation on Exercise Two: If you find your attention wanders during this Exercise, or you are unable to accommodate the intensity of it at times, remember to keep breathing rhythmically. Your breathing will always help to connect you with the physical plane.

You can also do this Exercise in another way: Instead of directing both hands towards the infant using Hand Position A, keep one hand facing palm upward during the entire process (Hand Position B). This will connect you even more strongly upwards to spirit, and will prevent you from losing sight of the spiritual connection which is the purpose of the Exercise.

You may find that one hand has a dominant role in the radiation process. In this case, visualize the current flowing **out** of this hand and into the baby, through the baby and back **into** the other hand, after which it flows upwards to Heaven.

The hand that is dominant while offering radiance will not necessarily be the one that is dominant in earthly tasks. You may be left handed as a rule, yet feel that your right hand is dominant when allowing energy to flow through.

Alternately, you may sense that one hand is dominant during one phase of the process, but when you move on to another stage of meditation, dominance shifts to the other hand. Your sensitivity to the currents of Spirit increases with practice, and you will become easily aware of these subtle energy differences.

Chapter

6

Radiance to the Pineal: The Spirit of the Crown

Physical and Spiritual Manifestations

The uppermost chakra is commonly referred to as the crown chakra. Correlations have been made to the haloes often depicted around the heads of holy figures in ancient art. The crown chakra is often represented as a golden globe of light above the head.

The physical point of correlation for the crown chakra is the pineal gland. This is a small ductless gland in the center of the cranial cavity, between the left and right lobe of the brain.

No clear physiological purpose has been found for the pineal body, although there are several theories. It was long thought to be "vestigial" organ – of no practical use! In the nineteenth century surgeons were in the habit of cutting out organs for which they could see no use. Fortunately the pineal escaped attention as it is almost completely inaccessible by normal surgery – it hangs right between the lobes of the brain.

The spirit associated with the pineal body is the Spirit of Love. The Spirit of Love is the supreme spirit, from which all else proceeds. The Spirit of Love encompasses all the Spirits below it. It is the primary connection with the divine. While this point is connected upwards, our physical body has life. When this connection is severed, it dies.

The pineal represents the transcendence point at which the unmanifest realm of spirit first becomes manifest as form. The Meditations in the following chapters are for use in conjunction with Exercise Two in Chapter Five. Radiance Meditation One starts with the joint between head and neck, the crossover point, and Meditation Two picks up with the pineal gland. Exercise Two in Chapter Five can be done with any or all of the Radiance Meditations in subsequent chapters.

•••••

Radiance Meditation One: The Crossover Point; the Junction of Heaven and Earth (Atlas and Axis Vertebrae)

Become aware of your breathing. Slow each breath to the point where you are conscious of every part of the path the air travels in and out of you. Become so attuned to the energy of your breath that you can sense every molecule as it passes in and out of your system. With each inbreath sense your connection to spirit. Draw the energy of your divine truth in with each inbreath. Center your mind, your thoughts, your whole attention on radiant love.

As you breathe out, feel your personal presence grow stronger. With each outbreath feel the potency of your spiritual presence increase. Feel the strength of radiance which you reflect intensify. Become fully and powerfully you.

Focus the energy moving through you by pointing your hands (Hand Position A). Place your hands on either side of the point represented by the top of the baby's neck. This is the location of the Atlas and Axis vertebrae, upon which the head pivots on top of the spinal column. Feel the energy pour from your hands into this area.

This point represents the junction between Heaven and Earth. Heaven is the realm of control, symbolized here by the head. The Earth is the place of response, response to the will and patterns originating in Heaven. It is represented by the torso. When this crossover point is clear of obstructions and functioning properly, the essences of Heaven pour through it into the Earth.

Visualize this crossover point being a clear unobstructed channel for the spiritual essences of your baby to move into form. Allow the love that pours from your fingers to gently dissolve any blockages in this channel. Sense the divine energy moving clearly and freely through this pathway and into the physical form. Hold your hands over this point in the same position until you sense that there is a clear and unobstructed flow through this point. The flow should be continuous and *stable before you move on.*

When you sense that this flow is consistent, move your hands gently to a point that represents the top of the baby's head. Keep your hand movement smooth, being very conscious that you are touching the sacred spiritual body of another being.

Radiance Meditation Two: The Spirit of Love: The Pineal Gland

Move your hands slightly in the general area of the baby's head until you sense, using your spiritual eyes, that you have made firm contact with the baby's pineal. Picture a stream of light pouring from your hands into the gland. It is a laser-like, brilliant white beam of love. It stimulates the area and cements the connection with the stream of God's love coming into the baby's head from above.

See the stream of vibrant energy that pours down from Heaven through the top of the baby's head, connecting the child to God. Caress this beam of light. Love the connection that this beam makes between the divine all, the Tao, and the earthly form. Cradle this energy beam in your hands as you celebrate its connection with the physical contact point available in the pineal.

Feel these intentions move through you into the child:

'You are love. Love underlies every other aspect of your functioning. Love is the essence of your nature. Love is what you live for. It is this constant love stream coming from God that

sustains your physical life. If this silver cord were not present, your physical form would cease to be alive. This column of love-substance penetrates your whole body and every part of it. It penetrates every other endocrine gland and energy point below it. It is the supreme principle of the universe, to which all else must be connected to survive. Always refer everything else in your whole life back to love, my dearest one. This is your constant reference point.

'In this moment I join my love to your love, allowing our columns of love to blend. They become more intense as they reinforce each other. In this moment I affirm my connection with the Divine. It is only because of my connection with the divine that I have anything to offer you. Affirming the solidity of my own spiritual centering allows me to direct and focus this current of love coming to you. Know, my child, that this love does not come from me in a personal sense. It is given freely by God, and as I open my heart and receive it into myself, it is mine to give freely.

'You will never be short of love. There is no scarcity of love. You do not have to hoard love, or be afraid that if you love certain people you will not have enough left over for others. You cannot claim love or possess love. You can only give love. As it is given, it overflows in the heart of the giver. God is love. God is infinite. Therefore love is infinite. I celebrate in this moment your connection with God in love.'

Once you sense that the flow of love is as fully received as it can possibly be by the baby's form, slowly move your hands to the next contact point.

Chapter

7

Radiance to the Pituitary: The Spirit of the Womb

Radiance Meditation Three: The Spirit of Truth: The Pituitary

Be aware of how deeply relaxed your body is. Breathe deeply. With each inbreath, breathe in a shining white radiance. With every outbreath, feel yourself coming more and more to focus. Feel this energy that you channel becoming more and more focused, more and more intense.

Move your hands to a point that represents the center of the baby's head – check the location of the pituitary gland on the chart in Chapter Five if you aren't sure. Use your spiritual eyes to see where this point is. Feel a steady stream of radiance emerge from your fingertips and into the pituitary. Allow your mind to be flooded with the Spirit of the Womb. Be acutely conscious of the atmosphere of nurturing, safety and protection that you are creating.

The Womb is the place in which life is created. As you are able to create the vibrational space in which life may grow, life will pour forth in your experience. The womb in which life of born is the Womb of Truth. In the Womb of Truth, the seed of Love is fertilized. The product of their union is Life.

Picture your baby developing in a manner that is utterly true to the inner reality. Let there be no deviance from the perfect focus of truth in any way.

The pituitary is also known as the master gland, as the hormones it secretes affect the secretion of hormones by other glands. Picture the control factors that are created by this master gland being true to the truth.

With the Spirit of the Womb of Truth filling your mind, allow the current of truth moving under the dominion of the Spirit of Love through your hands to increase. Allow the current of truth to intensify. With every breath you breathe out, breathe the spirit of truth into the baby's heart and mind. Allow this master gland in your own brain to move into the Spirit of perfect Truth. Keep it there unwavering. Feel the infinite love coming down from above igniting all truth in your heart and filling your understanding with discernment of truth. Hold yourself steadfast in the current of God's truth flowing out of Heaven in each moment.

Visualize a radiant line of connection drawn between this focus point of truth in your own brain and the brain of your baby. As you become steadfast in truth, so the child cannot be other than steadfast in truth. As you make room in your consciousness for nothing other than truth, harboring no deceit, no lies, no deception, no double-mindedness, the radiance of sanctity will surround even your physical form. The truth of love will uplift and bless every part of your emotional, mental and physical world.

As you recognize your own sacredness, your child will see God in the flesh. As your form becomes God's temple, the child will always have a place to worship. As your experience becomes the womb in which the Spirit of Truth always dwells, the child will grow up in safety. The Womb of Truth is the most precious gift you can give in which to nurture your baby.

Once this spirit has come to full radiant focus through your fingers pointed toward the pituitary gland of the child, become aware of your inbreath and your outbreath. You are breathing in the love of God and breathing out His truth as it is expressed through your form.

Chapter

8

Radiance to the Thyroid: The Spirit of Life

Radiance Meditation Four: The Spirit of Life: The Thyroid

The thyroid gland is located close to the Adam's apple (the bulge in the center of the throat) The thyroid is the physical focus of the Spirit of Life.

Move your hands down the child's body to a point that represents the front of the throat. With pointed fingers directing the flow of energy, make contact with this point. Use your sensing of the invisible currents of spirit to direct you accurately to this location.

As well as regulating the body's metabolic rate, the thyroid gland secretes a hormone essential to physical growth. This is merely the physical manifestation of the spiritual focus of the thyroid: to provide a physical contact point for the expression of the Spirit of Life

into the body.

Life is a force that bursts forth irresistibly when the Womb of Truth is exposed to the steady stream of the current of Love. Life does not have to be engendered or deliberately created. It is like the spark that is given off when a positive and negative pole touch each other. The spark does not have to be created in and of itself; it is a sure consequence of the interaction of positive and negative currents.

In the same way, Life bursts forth automatically when Love and Truth are in place. Life is irrepressible. In the springtime, unable to contain herself any longer, nature bursts forth with an incredible proliferation and profusion of fresh, shining forms. Nature's innate desire to create can, at a certain point, no longer be suppressed by winter, and bursts forth to transform the whole world. In the same way, when the Father of Love and the Mother of Truth are honored, the Child of Life cannot help but be born.

This child is a sacred representation of this principle at work. The life in this child does not need to be created by our conscious minds. We can do nothing from a self-centered point of view to encourage the growth of this child. We can only step back and let life have its way. If life is allowed to have its way, it is perfectly capable of organizing all the myriad, complex factors required in order to create a baby. It does not need an instruction book to do this. Ordered creativity is inherent to life. Life orders and organizes, and when we allow an increase of life in our personal experience it brings with it the gifts of purpose, ease and organic organization.

As your hands direct love to the area of your

baby's body which represents the thyroid gland, picture this infant bursting with life, with vigor, with joy, with the irrepressible exuberance of new life. Picture life as a glittering stream of energy surrounding the entire planet and permeating all its creatures. The amount of this sacred life-energy which we allow into our bodies determines how full our experience of life will be.

Picture this life energy flowing through the child's body without obstruction. Now picture the quantity of this life-energy increasing. Feel the pace of life within the child quicken, as the life-energy pouring through your focused hands intensifies. Feel the potential that this brings.

As this increased flow of the life current passes through the child's body, it nurtures and sustains the child; it enriches the child's experience. Rather than a miserable restricted trickle of life passing though the child, picture a gushing stream of life substance flowing though the child's body. Allow your focused hands to facilitate the increase of this flow. As you send these sparkling granules of life-energy coursing through the child's body, imagine them coursing more and more strongly through your own body too.

You cannot give what you do not have. Only as you allow an increased expression of the life current though your own experience will you be able to share with the child with this immeasurable gift of life. Imagine your own body filled to capacity with these flowing, brilliant granules. Imagine the pleasure God has in seeing one His creatures so filled with life, and so willing to pass it on to their child.

Once you feel a strong steady quality to this current

of life zipping through the physical body of the child, hold your hands steady for a few moments to allow this pattern to become stably implanted. Become aware of your breathing. With each exhalation feel the intensity of the life-field increase. When you sense the pattern is complete, move on to the next physical contact point.

Chapter

9

Radiance to the Thymus:
The Spirit of Purity

Radiance Meditation Five: The Spirit of Purification:
The Thymus

The spirit of purification is of vital importance in the age in which we live. We are in the midst of an Age of Purification in which the old ways are passing away. The old human order created by the mind of man divorced from God, is plodding its last doddering steps towards the grave. The new world, which the babies of the future are responsible for stewarding, is coming into manifestation. At this point the human race as a whole has chosen life, rather than the extinction which would have been certain had we hitched our awareness to the old order and followed it into oblivion.

The interim period – before the full manifestation of

the coming age – is a period of transition. The earth is being purified. The mechanism by which this takes place is the purification of the Heaven. As the new Heaven takes form the earth cannot help responding and following suit.

Our responsibilities, as awakened representatives of the new order, are NOT to try and tamper with or change the earth. Our spiritual responsibility is to change the Heaven, the Heaven of our own consciousness. It is in the invisible realms that the purification takes place first. Once the purification has taken place in spirit, the world of form will follow effortlessly. We never, never, never need to try to manipulate form. If the spirit is right the form will follow.

The time of purification is the time in which many of the old forms will pass away. If we are attached to form we will pass away with them. If our choice is to be with spirit we will be agents of the renaissance of spirit. There is a vast mass of material that requires transmuting in the fire of love. All the old creations of the human mind must go through the fires of purification to determine whether they are fit to exist in the new world.

We as a human race have created a great deal of stuff that does not belong, and which will not survive the purification process. Everything must go through the purification process in the next few years. For this reason our spiritual and physical facilities of purification are extremely important in the coming period. The thymus glands bring this spirit to particular focus in the physical body.

As you direct the life current from your hands into the area of the child's thymus, picture this area as a filter through which all the things in the old earth must pass on their upward ascent. Only things which are right and pure and fitting can pass through the filter of purification to become part of the New Earth. The fire of love burning in the filter of purification incinerates all those things which have no place in the New Earth.

Anything at all that comes through your child's system must pass through the filter of purification. Anything polluting, anything poisonous, anything disruptive, anything that is less than the best that comes into your child's system will be incinerated by the Spirit of Purification. Picture your child remaining pure no matter what temptations, distortions, or negative influences might bombard it. See nothing being able to touch it which is not for the best.

Picture your child being able to walk through the very worst problems that you could ever imagine, and in shining purity emerge unscathed on the other side. Picture this child with a passion for purity which allows nothing unclean to enter in.

As you hold your hands steady over this point in the child's body, feel the Spirit of Purity take root and grow strong in the child. When you sense that this spirit is firmly rooted, move on to the next contact point.

Chapter

10

Radiance to the Islets:
The Spirit of Blessing

Radiance Meditation Six: The Spirit of Blessing: The
Islets of Langerhans

If your child is a conduit for Radiant Love nurtured in the Womb of Truth, blossoming forth abundant Life and walking in perfect Purity, this child will bless the whole earth. The spirit of blessing is a natural consequence of looking upon the face of God.

The blessed individual does not only receive blessing from God, the blessed individual IS a blessing from God. The blessed person spreads blessing wherever they walk. Every hair on the head of the blessed one blesses the earth. Every breath the blessed one breathes out, by mingling with the air on this planet, extends the radiance of God into the Earth. The one who is blessed cannot help but bless. The blessed one is so focused on giving blessing that there is no need to look for blessing. In the presence of a blessed one, blessing simply is.

Not only are the fellow human beings of a blessed one blessed, but God is blessed. Honor is given to God by the presence of a blessed one.

In the old earth, blessing is seldom an inevitable product of human interaction. Looking at the total number of encounters in the humanly created old world, there are very few in which the participants feel blessed. In the new earth, however, blessing is the inevitable by-product of every single interaction between human beings. Living in love, guided by truth, bursting with life, the men and women of Heaven cannot help but bless each other.

The Spirit of Blessing comes to a particular physical manifestation in the Islets of Langerhans. The Islets are a collection of endocrine cells dispersed throughout the pancreas. The pancreas is found adjacent to the ribcage, where the left elbow joint meets the torso.

Direct the energy flowing from your fingers towards a place on your child's body representing the Islets of Langerhans in the pancreas. As you do this, feel the Spirit of Blessing moving out from you with every outbreath. Allow the current of blessing to intensify and move more strongly through your hands each time you breathe out.

Fill your mind with the blessing this child will convey to every person they touch or even think of. Picture this child blessing the earth and the natural world by their care and respect for spirit. Envision the pleasure God takes in the life of one who seeks to be a blessing to Him. Keep allowing this current of blessing

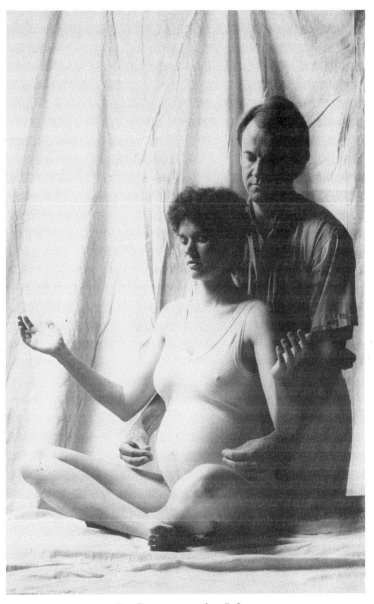

Radiance to the Islets

to build each time you breathe out. Sense the current of blessing become strong and stable in the child. Hold this feeling for a few moments in quietness. Be blessed yourself by the blessing this child will be.

When you sense that the pattern of blessing is stable and strong in the child, move on to the next contact point.

Chapter

11

Radiance to the Adrenals:
The Spirit of Purpose

Radiance Meditation Seven: The Spirit of Purpose:
The Adrenal Glands

*Become conscious once again of your breathing.
Each time you breathe out feel the steadiness of your
own life field. Feel the still point within you which is
aligned with the Spirit of Love. When you feel your
centering is as unwavering as the flame of a candle in
a still room, move your hands down the child's body to
a point which represents the adrenal glands. Use your
spiritual sight to make accurate contact with this
point.*

*The hormone secreted by the adrenals brings the
whole body into a heightened state of preparation for
action. The spiritual essence of which this gland is the
physical manifestation is the Spirit of Purpose. A child*

who embodies the Spirit of Purpose moves steadily toward their goal. They are not distracted by their emotional compulsions, their mental confusion, their bodily wants, cravings and additions.

The purposeful one is in control. The purposeful one is not pushed hither and yon by circumstance. The purposeful one is never 'under the circumstances.' The purposeful one acts in accordance with creative principle no matter what the circumstance is. No outside factors can disturb the Womb of Truth in which creation may take place.in the world of the purposeful one. The eyes of the purposeful one are always fully directed at what they are looking at. The purposeful one is always fully in the moment, fully in control of their own incarnational vehicle.

The purpose served by the purposeful one is simple and constant: to worship God and to serve the whole of life. For the purposeful one, there are no agendas other than love and service. The purposeful one is characterized by singleness of purpose. In singleness of purpose, human wants and distractions are never allowed to control. The purposeful one never neglects messages coming from body, mind and heart, but also never lets those messages dictate behavior.

What dictates behavior of the purposeful one is the creative pulsation of the moment, as it comes down from God out of Heaven. With eyes fixed singly on this goal, the purposeful one can bring the reality of Heaven into manifestation on earth. The purpose of the purposeful one is never to attempt to please man. With singleness of mind the purposeful one directs their effort to pleasing God.

Only when there is double-mindedness and dis-

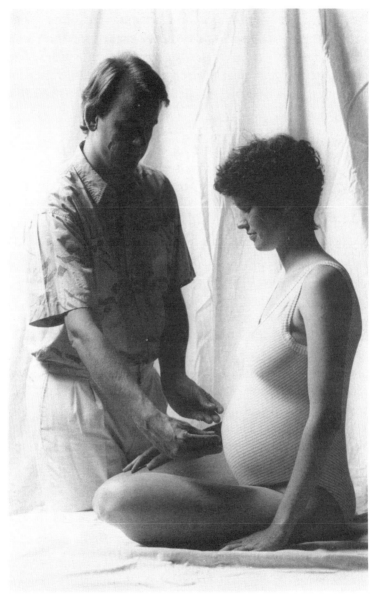

Radiance to the Adrenals

traction is a person's vision fragmented, and fear enters in. *Deceit and lies can never enter into the mind of one whose vision is singly centered in spirit. The vision of the one whose mind is purposefully fixed in spirit is radiant. It blesses all that it touches. When the fullness of divine purpose is known, the pettiness of human purpose becomes apparent and fades away.*

Using your breath as a guide, allow the current of the Spirit of Purpose to intensify in the radiation from your hands. Sense this spirit becoming fixed in the child. Welcome the Spirit of Purpose into the spiritual womb of the baby.

As you hold your hands above the adrenals in open welcome of the Spirit of Purpose, see the child moving in a straight line through life. Whatever the choices the child may have; whatever crossroads of experience the child may come to, see them choosing always the one which leads to the highest expression of divine purpose on earth. See them meeting the fog of doubt, disappointment and dismay and moving through it with the steadiness of purpose known by one whose heart is centered in divine knowing.

Give thanks for the singleness of purpose of this child. Give thanks for the singleness of purpose with which its body is now growing in the womb. Know that it will bring this same singleness of purpose to its mental growth, its emotional growth, its growth of understanding of its own spiritual nature. May the purpose of this child be to shine the light upon the earth.

When you sense a steadiness of radiance in this spirit, move to the next contact point.

Chapter

12

Radiance to the Gonads:
The Spirit of The Earth

The final endocrine glands, going from top to bottom, are the gonads. These are paired: in men, the testicles; in women, the ovaries. The Spirit associated with these endocrine glands is the Spirit of the New Earth.

•••••

Radiance Meditation Eight: The Spirit of the New Earth: The Gonads

Move your hands to the next contact point. Keep this movement smooth and fluid, bearing in mind that your hands are touching the vibrational sphere of another being. Sense when your hands have found the physical point that represents the gonads on the child's body. Envision the stream of bright love energy pouring from your hands into this point, and invoking the Spirit of the New Earth. With each outbreath, picture the flow of energy to this area becoming strong and stable. Welcome the Spirit of the New Earth into your own heart and mind.

The Heaven is the aspect of human function out of which creation springs. The pattern of control, for the past several millennia, has come from the human mind, dominated by the human heart, both divorced from the creative process. This state has run contrary to the purposes of life on earth. Man acting out of step with the rest of creation has produced his own creations; these often work at cross purposes with nature. This is the earth that has sprung from the humanly created Heaven. This earth is obviously a mess.

However, trying to change the earth while keeping the old heaven in place – the old state of consciousness intact – is useless. It is not the outside world that needs to be changed; it is the state of consciousness of human beings. When right spirit is in place, right creation results. All humankind's efforts to improve the earth while retaining the dominion of the old ways of thinking, the old heaven, cannot be successful.

When the New Heaven is permitted to come into place, the New Earth follows rapidly. When human motivation springs from the place of being, the work of being is done on earth, and the earth is renewed. Life-serving actions result, replacing self-serving actions.

The New Earth follows automatically when all the other factors of spiritual control are present. No effort is required to ensure that the outer factors of the child, the earthly factors, are pleasing. They will automatically be appropriate if they are designed by Heaven

112

and allowed to take form according to Heaven's blue-print. The New Earth then reflects the glories of the New Heaven.

The New Earth, as it comes into form, is a celebration of the qualities of the New Heaven. Our children will be agents, ministers of divine beauty in the earth. They will shed light by the very quality of their presence, and their actions will bring beauty. They will no longer be dominated by the old habits of mind and heart that enslaved past generations. They will no longer be bound by the boundaries which prohibited our generation from being all that we could be.

They will live without boundaries. None will be required, because the presence of spirit welling up from within co-ordinates the whole. Each piece finds its perfect place in the pattern of the whole of life.

Children of the New Earth will find themselves listening for their cues not to peers, parents, habits, addictions, or media, but to their inner voices, the messages that come to them from the Great Spirit. As they respond to these, they will renew the earth without trying, without striving. They will renew it simply by existing. The New Heaven, when it is established in the hearts of children, will create the New Earth.

Give thanks for the privilege of associating with this new child, bringer of the New Earth. With each breath welcome the Spirit of the New Earth into the form of this child. Feel the Spirit of the New Earth becoming firmly implanted in the child's vibrational realm. When you sense that this flow is steady, gently move your hands on to the next contact point.

Chapter

13

Radiance to Special Areas

There are several specialized areas which benefit from radiation, although they are not endocrine glands. Once we have established a steady flow of current through the endocrine glands, we can turn our attention to these other areas.

Hot Spots

During this phase, we can also use our sensitivity to spirit to locate any areas of the fetus' body that require special attention. This process is analogous to sensing, perhaps, that an adult has a bad back, or a faulty liver. We may "see" these factors with our spiritual eyes. Our hands may pick up a pattern of turbulence, or disturbance of the energy flow. Such areas may feel "hotter," or icy "cold" as we move our hands over them. During the process of radiance we give these areas attention once the endocrine pattern is completed.

Infinite Connections

We can also offer radiation through one person to another. This whole process works unhindered at any distance. These Meditations can be done by the parents of a young child who is temporarily away from home. This is an excellent way to maintain a connection with an absent loved one. It is not dependent upon proximity in either time or space.

Radiance can also be offered to a fetus using the mother's body as the point of connection. In this case, attunement is given to both mother and child simultaneously. The same applies to the father.

Couples who share this kind of an attunement with each other regularly know that this is perhaps the most precious time they ever spend together. It communicates feelings and sensings too deep to be expressed. Our spirits can speak at a level far beyond words. Even the words "I love you" presuppose an "I" and a "you" – a state of separation.

In the current of radiance there is no separation, for no words are necessary. In this state we cannot fail to be aware of the underlying oneness of all things. The illusion of separateness is demonstrated by spirit, as it crosses freely between physical forms, hearts and minds in order to do its life-affirming work. Spirit knows no boundaries.

Radiance is also a useful practice for situations in which you are with people who are stressed. You don't

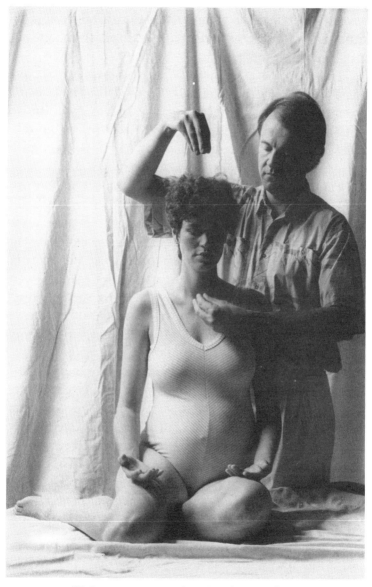

Using contact points in the Mother;
Radiance to the Thymus with Pineal as contact point

117

have to say anything in order to have an impact on the situation. Radiance will offer a soothing influence to the inflamed mind and heart.

This applies equally well to your own mind and heart when they are disturbed. If you get yourself into a state of spiritual distress, you aren't in a position to offer anything creative to anybody! Radiating to our own mind and heart reminds us of our spiritual origins. It centers us in the deepest core of our nature.

The ninth Meditation celebrates connection. We are all connected on the spiritual level to many other people. Through these spiritual connections we communicate constantly with others on an unconscious level. It is rather like a telephone switching station, with lines radiating out all over the place. What happens in the consciousness of the operator travels over all the lines simultaneously, to all the other people on our network.

When these kinds of messages come to us from people to whom we are connected, we may inexplicably feel depression, elation, fear, distress, or any number of other sensations and emotions. We pick up whatever they feel. If we are centered in right spirit, we simply send love back down the line. As creative beings, we choose not to reciprocate the distress! The ninth Meditation deals with this special ability of living beings to interconnect with one another in a radiant spiritual network.

•••••

Radiance Meditation Nine: The Spirit of the World; The Frontal Lobes

Moving your hands carefully and respectfully through the child's vibrational substance, go to a point representing the upper front portion of the head, around the temples. Behind this area of the skull are the frontal lobes of the brain, the seat of much of our individuality and personality. Open your hands once again (Hand Position B) *as though you were cradling the front of someone's head. Allow your heart to fill with thanks for the individual nature of this precious child-to-be. Picture this one's individuality being expressed to the fullest and highest potential possible. Picture spirit breathing life into the individual nature of this child, nurturing it to become all it can possibly be.*

Give thanks for the people that this child has already touched simply by existing. Give thanks for every contact it will have with other people throughout its life. Give thanks for the blessing this child will bring through everything it thinks, says, and does. Treasure the preciousness of this child. Feel the substance of its world as it radiates from the frontal lobes out to your fingers and hands. Feel the intensity of the creative process going on within.

Allow the pressure of connection between you to build. As you cradle this sphere of spirit within your hands, picture strands of spirit going out to touch all the people this child will ever meet. Sense how these channels of connection with others will be conduits through which blessing may move out from this child. It will touch those who are connected with this strand

119

whether or not their conscious mind is aware of it or whether the child is aware of it. Through our strands of connection with others we allow the spirits in our hearts to move out far beyond ourselves and affect hundreds of other individuals.

Feel your hands touching and blessing the child's entire world. Feel your hands touching and blessing the child's entire life. Feel the radiant current that comes from your hands touching and blessing every single person this child will every think about, talk about, be with or even glance at. When you have allowed the spirit of love to move through you fully to all these people, gently move your hands to the next contact point.

•••••

Radiance Meditation Ten: Areas Needing Special Attention

Moving very slowly, move your hands down the child's body. Feel how different areas of the body emit different vibrations. You may sense certain areas in which there is great vibrational activity and other areas which are more dormant. Using your spiritual sight, and the sensitivity to vibrations of your hand, see whether there are any areas of the child's body other than the endocrine glands which need radiation.

You may sense that a certain organ requires attention: you may pick up a particular mental or emotional trait which needs to be brought under the dominion of spirit. You may feel that everything is working just fine. Whatever the case, it is appropriate to use your

120

spiritual sensitivity to check out the vibrational patterns and to offer radiation wherever it is required.

When you sense that there is a pattern of disturbance or turbulence or particular intensity around a certain organ or system, hold your hands over that place and maintain a steady current of radiation until

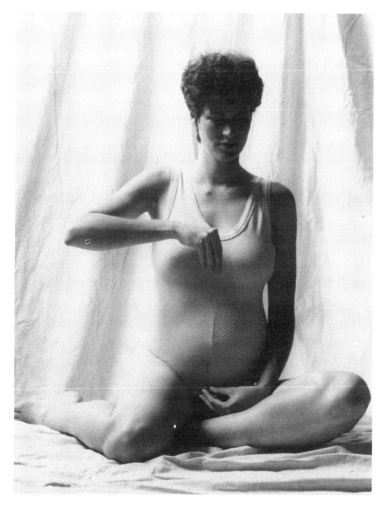

you sense that the vibrational pattern is stabilized, or until you sense that you have done as much as you can in that area. This may be a few moments or half an hour. Use your innate sensing to tell you how long to dwell on each place. Again, you are not trying to 'fix' anything, but rather are sharing a cycle of love in each of these areas with the child.

Even if you sense that no particular area of the child's body is in turmoil, just radiate up and down the whole physical form, giving thanks for its perfection. With each outbreath, let the baby feel your love and appreciation. As you move your hands over the child's body, become acutely conscious of the silver thread that connects you upwards to Heaven and allow the creative energy pouring down this thread to bathe and encompass the child. As it is physically bathed in placental fluid, let its spiritual womb be bathed in the substance of love. The substance of love washes away all fear, and lets the processes of creation take place in all their flawless perfection.

•••••

Radiance Meditation Eleven: Mind and Heart

Picture the heart, the emotional realm of the baby. Picture this heart being still, and free of turmoil. Envision this child enjoying the gift of stillness of heart all its life long. May its stillness of heart be oil upon the troubled waters of human emotion; may it be able to see the unrippled reflection of the hearts of others in the still pond of its own quiet heart.

May its heart overflow with joy and giving and

122

honesty. May the gift of its heart enrich the lives of those it meets. As the love of God pours down from Heaven to bathe this heart, may it overflow with love for others. May the love of God so fill this heart that there is no room for fear, anger, doubt, jealousy, resentment. May all negative emotions be washed away by the springing fountain of this heart's love.

Picture your child's love as a rich stream pouring forth in unending blessing. When this steam feels constant and secure, move your consideration to the child's mind. Allow an image of peace and stillness to fill your mind. Picture your child always having the gift of clarity of thinking, never being swayed by subconscious compulsions, emotional outbursts, or unthinking habits.

Let this child's mind dwell only on the light. As it dwells on the light, it becomes the bearer of the light; the bringer of divine light into the affairs of men. May the clarity of its perception guide this child through all the deceptions and pitfalls of the old world. May its wisdom illuminate the new Heaven and the new Earth.

When you sense through your hands that the pattern of clarity of mind and stillness of heart is firm and stable in the child, move your hands to the final contact point.

•••••

Radiance Meditation Twelve: The Spirit of the Crossover Point, Revisited

Move your hands gently back to the point where you first began to offer radiation: at the base of the skull; the atlas and axis vertebrae. Hold your hands in such a way that they focus the beam of your vibration-energy (Hand Position A). This point represents the junction between the New Heaven and the New Earth. This is the point through which the qualities of Heaven flow through into the earth. This is the point through which all the spirits move from potential into manifestation. Picture this channel being clear of any obstruction, and wide enough to let the fullness of this child's spirit move down into its form.

Hold this vision for a few moments until this channel is working swiftly and efficiently. When you feel that this is so, become aware of your breathing. Feel with each outbreath spirit flowing into form. As you inhale, absorb all the intensity of God's love flowing down out of Heaven through the connection through the top of your head.

Spend a few moments allowing this energy to move where it needs to move. Absorb the sparkling rain of energy into every particle of your being. Feel it refreshing you and re-invigorating every cell in your body. Give thanks for the strength and potency of this divine connection. Give thanks for being one of those who has the privilege of consciously knowing their divine connection.

Ask in your heart if there is anything else that Spirit would have you know. Know that you can dwell in this state of being, this state of grace and bliss, throughout the day, simply by becoming aware of the existence of it. Feel your body breathing in and out, in and out, in and out. When you are ready, open your eyes.

•••••

Attuning to the Implicate Order of Life

Spiritual contact with the unborn child ought to be an ongoing process. Parents should check in with the fetus at least once a day or more, just to make sure that all the vibrational patterns are developing smoothly. With experience, this process becomes almost instinctive.

This time of the day becomes a deeply sacred period of connection and affirmation of the child's spirit. It becomes something that one would neglect no more readily than feeding a child, or washing it. Once the importance of spiritual factors is recognized, these in fact become more important than the outer circumstances.

With practice, our eyes become sharp, our ears become tuned, to the spiritual nature of things. We no longer look for causes on the physical level. We seek the origins of things – emotions, events, diseases – on the invisible level at which they originate. The creative process always begins on the invisible level, and moves to the visible. After a time, we are no longer distracted by the visible, and do our most significant work in the realm of spirit.

The ability to pick up the invisible factors present in any situation becomes not second nature, but first nature. Our concern with manipulating the material world in order to secure our satisfaction fades into the past as we recognize that spirit already has the world under control: there is a pattern inherent in life itself. As we identify our outer selves – our incarnational vehicles of body, mind and heart – with life, that inherent order flows out through our actions. No manipula-

125

tion is required. Only trust is required, trust that life works. And that should be the first thing that having a baby teaches us: Life Works!

Chapter
14

Spiritual Responsibilities
of Father and Mother

Every common action has a mythic quality. When we as individuals repeat certain actions that millions of other individuals have done over time, we participate in the archetype of that particular action. The ancient Greeks represented archetypes in their literature in such a vivid way that they are still with us today: the Gorgon, Oedipus, Aphrodite, and so forth.

The Mother As Archetype

Parenting is a mythic event. A woman is not merely a single mother of a single child. Through childbirth, through simply being a woman, she participates in the myth of the Great Mother. The qualities of the Great Mother are known: infinite caring, inexhaustible tenderness, fierce protection of her young, bringing forth earth's bounty, replenishing the species, etc. A woman participates in these age-old realities simply by being.

The characteristics of these myths are passed from generation to generation. They are passed from mother to child. If they are weakly represented in the mother, they will be weakly represented in the child. If the mother is a strong example of the qualities of the Great Mother, there will be a strong image in the child's mind of what this means. Once implanted in the child's reasoning, these values come out in all the child's dealings with, and vision of, the world.

Part of the feminine model is the essence of caring. This great archetype, the Caring Mother, transfers readily from the child's consciousness into the child's relationships with other people, and with all living things. For example, a child with a strong assumption of the values of the Great Mother will be able to relate to our planet as the Earth Mother. Such a one could never harbor the idea that personal survival depends on exploiting the planet. The mental circuitry for this sort of assumption is simply not there. So destroying the environment for personal gain will not be an option for such a child.

In these sorts of ways we program into our children the assumptions we program into ourselves. If we remain unhealed ourselves, we cannot offer our children healing. Conversely, as we let ourselves be healed first, we are able to extend healing to our children. The actions of a healed one spread out with a ripple effect, and ultimately extend healing to the entire planet.

A healed child, with a vivid subconscious picture of the qualities of the Great Mother, will give all women the respect due the Great Mother. Such a child will see the Great Mother reflected in all women, and will honor them accordingly.

Earth Mother Represents Heaven Mother

To her children, the earthly mother is a representation of the Great Mother in living flesh. She is the Goddess made manifest. She is a flesh representation of the essence of Woman. She is a living monument, a walking icon of Godhead in its female form. If she faithfully represents this in all her actions, the child will be able to relate to all the other places in human relations where this archetype is found. If there is a void where this Goddess-image should be, there will be a void in relating to others in this way.

The Great Mother embodies the Spirit of the Womb. The womb in which life is born is the Womb of Truth. A true mother takes care to ensure that her actions always be true to the Truth of Being. Manifesting the Truth of Being in the world of the child, she provides a lifelong pattern for the child.

The pattern she exemplifies allows the child to connect with the Truth of Being wherever they may find it in later life. If this model is not placed in the child's consciousness by the mother, the child will have trouble recognizing Being when exposed to it later on. The true mother, by simply being fully herself, provides the child with a model of personal truth that endures throughout the child's life. The actions of the true mother create the conceptual circuits in the child's brain for recognition of Truth.

A childhood nurtured in the Womb of Truth will

translate into an adulthood that cherishes Truth. If the model of Living Truth is known, the child will be anchored against the force of all the distortions that arise from of the outside world, and the mass subconscious. If the Womb of Truth is nurtured in the child's life, that child will in turn beget the child of the Womb of Truth, which is Life. A child nurtured in the Womb of Truth is born into abundant life.

So true motherhood is not an everyday commonplace happening! It is an event of mythic proportions. In motherhood, woman becomes the living flesh representation to the child of Mother God, implanting in the child's awareness a recognition of Truth that will be a lifelong gift, an enduring anchor. Without this example, there will a void in the child's conceptual world where the image of Mother God should be.

Heavenly Father in Earthly Form

To his children, the earthly father is a representation of their Heavenly Father. A child is not adept at separating spirit from flesh. A child lives in the awareness of the union of the two: Heaven gives rise to earth, and earth ascends to Heaven; Heaven and earth are one. A child is not capable of reasoning: "Ah, now, my earthly father is doing these awful things, but my Heavenly Father would never do that." To the child, seeing Heaven and earth interchangeably, there is no bold line dividing earthly and Heavenly Father. The earthly father is the concrete flesh representation to the child of the Heavenly Father. The spiritual responsibility of the earthly father is to represent the qualities of the Heavenly Father accurately to the child.

The earthly father cannot create this model of Father God out of his own wisdom and strength. If he tries, he will fail miserably. He will be reduced to falling back on bluster, coercion and tyranny.

The only way in which an earthly father can represent Father God to his children is by becoming one with his Heavenly Father. The earthly father allows his personal ego to fade, his personal identity to diminish, to the point where he is transparent. When his earthly personality fades into insignificance as his full attention is turned to his Heavenly Father, he becomes one with his Heavenly Father. His earthly life becomes a transparency through which his Heavenly Father is clearly seen. The earthly father who has blended his identity in joyous union with his creator is a window through which the light of Heaven may shine.

The Focus of the Hero

How does the earthly father do this? By love. His paramount love is for his Heavenly Father. He shows his love for his Heavenly Father by doing His works, by the care he takes to be a faithful steward of his Heavenly Father's creation. Consumed in love for his Heavenly Father, his earthly personality fades into the distance. When others look at him, they see only the face of the Father within.

The face of response of the earthly father is not turned towards his wife, or his children, or anyone from whom he seeks advantage. His primary focus of love **is not those around him**. The face of his attention is instead turned always to the Heavenly Father within. When and only when the earthly father's response is

131

first and foremost to the Great Father, the love of the Great Father shines out from him to bless those around him.

To his children, the earthly father is the flesh representation of the Heavenly Father. As his children grow into understanding, they easily recognize the qualities of Heaven wherever in life they find them, for they have known from birth the representation of Heaven.

Boy children with such a father know what manhood is about, for they have seen the example of a man consumed with love for the things of Heaven. They have lived with a father though whose eyes they could look and see God. They know what true manhood means. They are not likely to be sidetracked by the violent, uncaring, macho stereotypes of "manhood" they will encounter in the mass culture.

Girl babies, as they grow up, also know what true manhood is about. They can sense it, or the lack of it, in the men they meet. For they have seen the form of their Heavenly Father shining through the presence of their earthly father. They are unlikely to be mislead by "men" who posture impressively; who talk grandly, who look good on the outside but are empty husks at the core. They are accustomed to seeing through a man. The earthly father welcomes anyone to see through him, for in doing so they can gaze upon the face of the Great Father within. Being "seen through" is no threat for the man whose response is anchored in the Father within.

The True Responsibility of Parents

With an earthly mother representing the Womb of Truth, and an earthly father representing the face of

Love, the child of Life can be born. The child of spirit filled parents has a complete spiritual education through witnessing the Being of its parents.

Once Being is in place, all other earthly skills required can be added. If Being is not in place, is not understood, then no matter how many earthly skills a child may acquire, the central core of that child will be shaky. Our present society teaches us to acquire goods and expertise. This is an unsatisfying attempt to substitute forms for the central reality of spirit.

The primary responsibility of the parent **is not** to give the child a good school, a nice house, etc. The primary task of the responsible parent is to represent spirit to the child. Children soon see if their parents' emphasis is on the inner reality, or outer forms, and begin to structure their own reality accordingly.

But forms do not bring security. Material goods do not bring security. What does bring security is knowing who you are, and knowing that who you are on the deepest level is God. Once the reality of God-Being is experienced, and the conviction of oneness with a friendly universe is absolutely fixed in place, then the child may remain a poor peasant, or sit in the councils of the mighty, and neither external condition will matter.

The only thing that matters to the child of God is that they live in God. There is no other reality. There is no other fulfilment. Parents who live in God represent the reality of God living in the flesh to their children. This is spiritual parenting.

•••••

Meditation:

For this Meditation, make sure you are in a quiet room and will not be disturbed. Low lights are helpful, as is quiet, meditative music. You can tape the Meditation and play it back to yourself, or use the Communing With the Spirit of Your Unborn Child tape, or you can have your partner or a friend read it to you.

Close your eyes. Let your whole body become still. Breathe deeply, and feel the tensions drain out of your body. Become aware of each inbreath and each out-breath. Visualize the tension in your body as a colored fluid, filling every part of you. As you breathe out, let more of this colored fluid out with every breath.

Start at your feet. With each outbreath, visualize the tension leaving your feet, breath by breath. Keep breathing out the colored tension-fluid until your feet are completely relaxed. Feel how empty and loose your feet are. Enjoy the feeling of emptiness.

When you have drained every molecule of tension out of your feet, and they are completely relaxed, start on your calves. Let the fluid filling your calves and ankles move out of you on your breath, breath by breath, until they are completely empty and relaxed. When every cell in your calves is relaxed, move on to your thighs.

Do this all the way up your body. Drain your shoulders of the colored tension-energy, letting them sag completely. Once you have breathed out all the fluid and they are completely relaxed, start with the top of your head and begin to breathe out all the tension in your head. Let all the struggles of this day recede. Let all the thoughts and concerns of this day glide gently out of your body as you breathe out. Take as many breaths as you need to let all the tension energy out of your head.

Then clear your mouth and neck, allowing the last bits of tension to flow out of you. Now, with your whole body limp and relaxed, let your attention drift down again to see if you have any pockets of colored tension-energy that linger still. Find those subtle areas where you are still tense, and allow these last lingering tensions to slip gently out of your body with each relaxed breath.

You are now an empty, relaxed physical form. Behind you, sense the beautiful radiant presence you are coming to know quite well. It is the real you, the angel that is the truth of your being. Take a moment to appreciate the beauty of your spiritual self. Feel your body being enfolded in the radiant presence of this loving spirit. Feel the wonderful sense of fulfilment and completion that comes when the inner you and the outer you become one.

Notice how your spirit-body is connected upward, a bright cord that comes out of the top of your head and reaches all the way up to Heaven. Through this cord, feel the love of Heaven flowing down to you. Feel your own thankfulness at being one with this wonderful being flowing upwards up the cord.

Once you have had ample time to enjoy the miracle of oneness, call up before you a series of images, like a movie of your life, scene by scene. Linger on those memories that are most vivid. Re-experience them fully. Feel what it felt like to be there. Remember all the feelings associated with each scene. Keep going back, further

135

and further, till you are a youth, a child, a baby. Go back to the earliest memories of childhood.

Think of an incident when you were a child, a time when you had a really great experience of meeting a wonderful man. Think of the man that impressed you most when you were very young. Just remember how awed you were to be meeting such a man. Remember the feeling of importance that the you had, just being in the presence of this man. Remember the feeling. Pause for a moment to re-create that feeling fully. Hold that feeling with you strongly.

Now imagine the light of connection shining down from Heaven on to this man's head, the light of connection to Father God. Visualize this man really loving you as a child, and treating you as though you were the most important person he had ever met. See his love for you. Visualize Father God's love pouring out to you through the eyes of this man. When you have a very strong picture of being loved and respected and treasured and honored in this way, let the image fade, but let the feeling of being loved and soothed by this wonderful man remain.

Now think back to another thing that happened when you were a child. Think back to the worst experience you had with an adult man. Think of the meanest, cruellest man, perhaps someone who abused you terribly, or perhaps someone who you just saw but knew was bad. Remember how frightened you felt. Remember how powerless you were against this awful man. Remember how small you were. Remember all the worst things that happened. Remember all the feelings that went along with those awful things you experienced.

136

Now picture the wonderful man coming down from above, into the place where you are with the horrible man. As he comes down, light comes from his body. He is looking at you with love. You feel his love. You feel all the wonderful things you felt before in his presence. You feel safe, secure, protected by his shining presence. You run to him and he embraces you and enfolds you safely in his shining presence.

You look back again at the horrible man, but he is fading away! As the light streams into the place from the beautiful man, the awful man is like a shadow that is just melting away. You can hardly see him anymore. There is nothing to be afraid of anymore! You feel how much stronger the power of the wonderful man is than that of the horrible man. You take the hand of the Great Father and walk towards where the awful man was. But there is nothing there anymore. He is like a dark shadow that faded away when the light of your True Father appeared. You look into the eyes of your father, and they are full of love for you. You know that he will always be there when you need him. You know he can always protect you. You know he can always dispel the forces of darkness.

Now go back to the movie of scenes from your life. Find a picture, a particular image, that represents your earthly father. It could be a photograph, or a particular memory, or even a feeling that you had when you were around him. Just choose something that sums up your father for you.

Now picture his face really closely. Picture looking into his eyes. Feel the feelings you felt when you were around him.

Now let his face and his eyes dissolve into the face

and eyes of the Great Father. Even as you are watching, the contour of his face changes and blends into the face of the Great Father. Feel the love your father had for you. Maybe he wasn't able to show it, maybe he never expressed it, but know that he was trying to love you the best he knew how. He may not have known the best way. But he was <u>trying</u>. Feel how much he wanted you to know how he loved you, even if he never showed it.

Feel yourself loving him back. Feel how full your heart is with the Great Father's love. Feel how loving you feel towards your earthly father, and how much you appreciate his having tried so hard. Feel your love just pouring over him. Feel how much the Great Father loves him. Feel the Great Father's love melting your daddy's heart. See his heart being caught up into the heart of the Great Father. Just watch, and give thanks, for as long as you like. Enjoy seeing your daddy and the Great Father become one.

Now go back to your movie of your life as a child. If there are any scenes you would like to go where there were bad experiences with men, feel the terror of them fully. Then allow your Great Father to be there with you, and feel the peace and serenity that comes from his presence. Know he will always be there for you. Turn the tape off till you are done with remaking your childhood men. You can turn it on again when you are ready to go on.

•••••

When you have remade as many scenes from your childhood as you like, think back to the most wonderful

138

experience with a woman that you had. Remember a time when you were very young, and were with a woman who you thought was just wonderful. Remember how awed you were at her presence. Remember how beautiful and graceful she seemed. Remember how good she was to other people. Remember how good that child that is you felt just to be with her. Keep feeling that feeling. Treasure that feeling in your heart, and keep it in your memory.

Now envision that stream of light from Heaven shining down on the top of her head, making her whole body glow with light. She becomes more and more beautiful as the light pours down upon her. Her face, her eyes, her hair, her body all shine with beauty.

Now picture her eyes turning to look at you, the child. They are the eyes of Mother God. You feel the Truth of who she is, you feel the absolute trust you have for her spirit. You feel how enfolded you are in her presence. Engrave this feeling on your heart.

When you have the feeling firmly fixed in your heart, let the image fade, and see your movie of your life once again. As you review the scenes, pick a time when you had a horrible experience with a woman as a young child. Picture the scene and remember how it was. Remember exactly what happened. Recall every detail of the scene, and just how bad it was. Remember how awful you felt inside.

Now see the Great Mother coming down from Heaven. As she comes down, the whole place where you are is filled with radiant light. Her presence brings a lightness, a joy, a perfection with it. You look at her and feel the awful feeling in your heart melting. She reaches her hand down to take yours, looking at you with love. You feel your heart jump up to be with her, to join with her.

You look back now to where the horrible woman was, but she is dissolving in the light coming from Mother God. Your fear has melted, and you walk towards her, but there is nothing but a shadow left. You walk right through the spot where she was. There is nothing there anymore.

You look up into the eyes of Mother God, and know that she will always be there for you, whenever you need her. You know that her Truth will dispel any falsehood, and you can call on the Great Mother to represent Truth to you whenever you are in doubt. Know that you will always be able to remember this feeling whenever you need it.

Now go back to your movie. Find an image that represents your earthly mother: a photograph, a scene, perhaps even an object. Find whatever it is that really represents your mother to you. Now feel the feelings that you associate with this image of your mother. Feel them fully. Feel the way you felt about her when you were a child. Remember the way she was towards you.

When you have this image of your earthly mother firmly in your mind, imagine a light coming from behind the image. It makes the whole image light. The image glows with radiance. Through the image of your mother shines the light of the Great Mother. Feel again how much the Great Mother loves you. Feel her love pouring to you through the image of your mother. Feel the spirit that you know is true of Mother God. Envision Mother God and your earthly mother blending into one.

Spend some time, now, to be with your earthly mother. See how hard she was really trying, despite the burdens that she had to deal with. See how the light was really shining inside her, although it was buried so much of the time. Let the light in you connect with the light in her, and let your two lights mutually reinforce each other.

When you have enjoyed some time with the true spirit of your mother, go back to the movie of your childhood. Remember any other miserable or frightening times you had with adult women. Be fully in them. Remember all the feelings they brought up in you. Then invoke the light of Mother God. Let Her be there in the situation with you. Feel again the feelings you have in Her presence.

When you have dealt with as many situations as you like, become aware of your radiant beam of connection upward with the light. Feel the light streaming down on you from Heaven. Let the essences of Mother God and Father God pour down into you with the light. Let the essence of Mother God take root in your heart. Find a special place in your heart where the essence of Mother God belongs, and put it there. Let this be the holy place you can always go back to when you need to remember the Great Mother.

Let the essence of Father God fill you as the light streams down from above. Let the essence of Father God take root in your heart. Find a part of your heart that belongs exclusively to Father God. Let the essence of Father God rest there, to blossom into your awareness whenever you need Him. Remember this most sacred place where God the Father will always live in you.

Keeping the intensity of this feeling with you, spend a few moments radiating the spirit of Father God and Mother God to people who you know who particularly need it. Think of friends and relatives who are not in touch with the spirit of either Father God or Mother God, or both, and visualize a current of your radiance reaching out to them; wherever they are on the surface of the planet. The distance doesn't matter. See the radiance touching their hearts, breathing into their experience the essences of Mother and Father God. Bless them with your radiance. Feel them bathed in your love.

When you are done, let the pattern of radiance come to rest. Feel your spirit become still again. Let the glow around you become regular and steady. Become aware of your breathing. Feel your breath travelling in and out. When you are ready, open your eyes. Let the way you feel at this moment stay with you the whole day. Look for ways to radiate the essence of Father God or Mother God to the people you meet. Go back to those two special places in your heart whenever you need to.

•••••

Unlimited Grace For Unlimited Healing

We can re-create the perfect father and the perfect mother within our own psyche, within our own lifetime. We do not have to bound by the imperfect stereotypes that we have constructed out of personal experience and the mass consciousness. Some of us as children had inadequate experience, miserable experience or no experience of what true earthly parents should be. There is a void in our psyche where these life-creating symbols should be. If this void remains, life will continue in us unfulfilled.

But this does not mean that we cannot restore these cornerstones to our lives. We don't have to live all our lives without the Great Mother and Father God, and the destructive effect this has on our personal relationships. The psychological scars inflicted upon us as children do not have to remain in our consciousness, where they are likely to be re-inflicted on our own children. We can be healed.

Father and Mother God exist in spirit even though they may not exist in form in our awareness. As we begin to live in spirit ourselves, we suddenly have access to all the things we lack in form. And as the spirit grows strong in our experience and becomes habit, becomes first nature, spirit begins to fill out the forms that our necessary. The desolate places of our experience are comforted. The weak places are made strong. Mourning becomes joy. Grief and lack are replaced by fulfilment and peace. We are rebuilt, reconstructed in Life's perfect image as we come close to Love and Truth.

We can be completely restored. That doesn't mean just being patched up enough to continue functioning. It means claiming the glorious fulness of life. The old scars in mind and heart can melt. Our innermost being can be transformed. As we live with Father and Mother God in spirit, their presence reaches down into form to transform our lives, our work, our relationships. If you didn't have this example represented to you by adults when you were a child, spirit can put it there. Spirit can overcome all things.

Once we are healed, and we learn to live our lives and go our way as spiritually responsible and mature adults, we look for opportunities to radiate spirit to others. As this becomes a natural and normal thing to do, a common habit, it has a powerful effect on the body of mankind.

Being God to the Child

Myths are the shared race memory of the species. As we live our lives as heroes and heroines, being God in our circumstances, the energy field created by our actions reinforces the whole energy field of similar actions on the planet. In this way, we co-create the new myths, the myths of humankind restored to its true position of oneness with God. As enough individuals change their own reality, the reality of the whole is changed, and the earth is returned once again to its creator.

As we as individuals take responsibility for being reborn ourselves, we offer the gift of immaculate conception to our children. They are no longer born just out of human heritage. As we allow ourselves to blend with God, we allow them to be born of spirit and flesh simultaneously, fruit of the union of God and man.

Chapter
15

Spirit-Filled Relationship

As the previous chapter discusses, healing of the child begins with healing of the parent. In order for the parent to extend wholeness to the child, the parent must be whole to start with. You can offer only what you have. The advent of a child is the catalyst for spiritual renewal in ourselves. As we consider birth, we must consider first of all our own rebirth.

The Power of Transcendent Relationship

A child, coming into the world full of potential, full of newness, is a living reminder of our own need for newness, an invitation to consider our own potential anew.

The fact that, in a spiritual relationship, the substance of both parents is required to create the climate for the birth of spirit into the world through a child, forces us as parents to re-examine our relationship with each other.

What is the quality of our being together? Do we put spirit first, or are we centered in the world of form? Are we objecting to the outer form of our partner's behavior, or are we discerning of the inner essences? A fetus growing in the inmost part of the body is a powerful symbol of the creativity that hides in the inner parts of us. Honoring the spirit of the unborn child is an expression of our desire to honor the most sacred parts of our own inner nature.

Relationships between men and women is one of the primary areas in which the most vivid contrasts of human behavior are found. They inspire people to the most noble and the most depraved behaviors. People can assume a pleasant veneer which suffices for casual social relationships, but those they live with day in and day out see the flaws that are hidden from general view. Partnering and parenting relationships thus go to the core of what we really are, to the roots of being.

Conversely, if we are able to have victory in these dark corners of our lives, the light that is released illuminates every other area more brightly. If the quality of our integrity stands up to the gaze of even those who have most frequent opportunity to witness our failures, we may stand tall indeed. It is in these relationships that our subtle weaknesses are exposed. They are consequently our most valuable proving ground for practical spirituality.

When your relationship with your partner is a transcendent one, it will be a source of deep power and affirmation on both the inner and outer level. Couples that have learned the lessons of living together with joy possess a magical resource infinitely more important than any outer possession.

These relationships are where the real spiritual work is done of restoring the earth to Life. They are the first place we demonstrate our degree of personal awakening. It is not the orators, swamis, preachers, and seminar leaders that do the great work of enlightenment. It is the people in the clinches: those who show the face of God to the world by their everyday actions, who stand in the checkout line at the supermarket with grace, who lubricate axle bearings with serenity, who clean up after bedridden patients with a spirit of love, who mow lawns with the voice of God singing in their minds.

The Veneer of Pleasantness

The quality of our most private relationships is not a hidden thing. It may not be visible to many people. But it shows up at the forefront of our spirit. Anyone can appear pleasant to a stranger. But how do you appear to your partner, first thing in the morning? Do you radiate love, acceptance, joy and peace? Are you an inspiration to the world with the first words you say? Are the first thoughts that you allow into your mind ones which bring Heaven into the earth?

Parenting brings all these things to point. To create a spiritual womb for the child, our own spirits must be clear. Clear creation is done through a clear spirit. A spirit contaminated with judgment, blame, criticism and accusation will contaminate the creations which spring

147

in to form through it. Remember, spirit underlies form. Form reflects spirit – faithfully. That is why trying to clean up displeasing forms is futile. If we pay attention to the quality of spirit that we put out, taking care that it is clear, then our creations in form will be clear. The radiance of spirit will shine through them.

What parent would not want the light of Heaven to shine through their child? The parent that wants this has a direct personal responsibility. The light of Heaven shines through the child when it is allowed to shine through the pure heart and still mind of the parent. And that means saying "No!" to all the dark things that rise up from within us to obscure our light, and cast a shadow upon our children.

These dark things are most often jarred loose by our most intimate personal relationships. Husbands and wives typically talk to each other in tones much less sensitive than those they employ with anyone else they know. They reserve their harshest criticism for each other. They feel a license to abuse each other that they are not granted by other relationships. They are short with each other, dismissive, and oblivious to change. They are often the first to resist and the last to notice growth in the other.

It is extremely paradoxical that in relationship with the ones we claim to love most, the veneer of civility is thinnest. We talk to them more rudely than to anyone else we know. And supposedly we love them the most! If closeness were judged by the way we talk to each other, an objective observer would conclude that our husbands and wives are the people we love least!

This is why these relationships are the most fertile field for spiritual renewal. It is no accident that these relationships are the closest to us. It is no accident that these are the people we are with most of the time. The reason for this close association is that this is where the real, deep spiritual work is done. **Life has designed things in such a way that we are presented with our most radical opportunities for growth in our most obvious relationships.** We don't have to climb the Himalayas to Lhasa. We don't have to crawl the Stations of the Cross. Our sanctity is shown instead by the way we treat those who are closest to us.

Our most sacred relationships are not those we have with our gurus, shamans, priests or pastors. Our most sacred relationships are those we have with our partners. They are designed to give us the most practice in being holy. They give us constant opportunities to transcend our petty emotions. The are full of room for the expression of the light-beings of spirit that we are. When we are expressing our light constantly in these relationships, we are truly filled with light.

How is this accomplished? By choice.

Choosing Love

Our choices are made in the moment. They are not made to cover the future. The future is the sum of all the instants that we create. It is by being light in these present moments that we shed light into the future.

In the moment that a situation comes up in which we are habitually inclined to show our fangs, we choose to show our halo instead. Each time we would instinctively lash out at our loved one, we choose instead to love.

The love is inside us, after all. The love is in fact the

truest part of us. Bitterness and anger may dwell in our hearts too. But expressing it only reinforces that habit pattern. **Every time we choose to love rather than choosing to fear, we strengthen the habit of love.** The sum total of our choices determines our character.

Negative habit patterns may be very deeply ingrained. Fortunately, we do not have to deal with the whole pattern at once. We only have to deal with the present moment. Each time that habit comes up, we have an opportunity to make our choice in that moment. We either say: "Yes, I will bow down and worship at the shrine of this habit by giving in to it" or we say, "I recognize this habit, and know it exists in a part of me. But I also know that in essence I am an angel. I choose to express the angel."

We choose what we express. And in time, we become what we express. The things we allow to come through us, mold us. As we begin to consistently choose the angel in each moment, that choice becomes a habit. We turn first to Heaven in any situation, because we have forgotten how to engage the negative emotions that once were our staple. The sum total of an infinite number of present moments becomes our weeks, our years, our lifetimes.

In choosing Heaven as the source of our actions, we begin to bring Heaven into the earth. We become identified with Heaven. As we drop the behaviors that are our human grave clothes, we become one with the nature of Heaven. "Heaven" no longer means an ephemeral afterlife. It is the stuff of everyday reality. Every day is filled with opportunities to express the character of Heaven. In this way, the earth is reclaimed for its Creator.

Resource Directory

The following resource list offers the opportunity to connect up with those who have an alive interest in natural childbirth and in daily living in alignment with life's values. If none of the following resources are in your area, you may contact any one of them to find out if there is someone in your local area to contact.

Glen Ivy
25000 Glen Ivy Road
Corona, CA 91719
(714) 735-8701

Toronto Attunement Center
3409 Yonge Street
Toronto, Ontario M4N 2M8
CANADA
(416) 440-4054

Vancouver Attunement Centre
2075 W. 37th Avenue
Vancouver, BC V6M 1N7
CANADA
(604) 263-7299

Huntington Wellness Center
202 Main Street
Huntington, NY 11743
Dr. Leonard Izzo
(516) 673-1014

Dr. Malcolm Williams
558 Main Street
South Portland, ME 04106
(207) 775-2265

Family Chiropractic Center
4804 Grover Avenue
Austin, TX 78756
(512) 458-5379

Green Pastures Estate
Ladd's Lane
Epping, NH 03042
(603) 679-8149

Attunement Center
910 70th Avenue, S.W.
Calgary, AB T2V 0P7
CANADA
(403) 258-1220

Victoria Attunement Center
#1 2727 Quadra Street
Victoria, BC V8T 4E5
CANADA
(604) 383-1243

Further Reading

The following is a selection of books on the topics discussed in this book. A few highly recommended titles can be ordered directly by using the order form in the back.

Marriage and Relationships:

Love is Letting Go of Fear, Gerald Jampolsky. Celestial Arts, 1979.

Magic At Our Hand; Releasing Our Lives Into Order and Beauty, Nancy Exeter. Foundation House, 1988.

A Shared Creation: The Meaning of Pregnancy, Dr. Paul Brenner. Saybrook, 1988

Marriage, Parenthood & Enlightenment, Swami Rama. Himalayan Institute, 1977.

Birthing:

Birth Reborn, Michael Odent. Pantheon, 1986.

Birth Without Violence, Frederick Leboyer. Knopf, 1975.

Birthing Normally: A Personal Growth Approach To Childbirth, Gail Peterson. Mindbody, 1984.

Childbirth Wisdom for the World's Oldest Societies, Judith Goldsmith. Congdon & Weed, 1984.

Childbirth With Insight, Elizabeth Noble. Houghton Mifflin, 1983.

Childbirth Without Fear: The Original Approach to Natural Childbirth, Grantly Dick-Read. Harper & Row, 1987.

Commonsense Childbirth, Lester Dessez Hazel. Berkeley, 1976.

The Experience of Childbirth, Sheila Kitzinger. Penguin, 1984.

Giving Birth: The Parents' Emotions in Childbirth, Sheila Kitzinger. Schocken, 1978.

Immaculate Deception–A New Look at Women & Childbirth, Suzanne Arms. Bantam, 1977.

Infant Massage: A Handbook For Loving Parents, Vimala Schneider. Bantam, 1982.

Special Delivery: The Complete Guide to Informed Birth, Rahima Baldwin. Le Femme Publishing, 1979. Celestial Arts, 1988.

Spiritual Midwifery, Ina May Gaskin. Book Pub. Co., 1978.

Water Babies: The Igor Tjarkovsky Method for Delivery in Water, Erik Sidenbladh. St. Martin, 1983.

Pregnancy:

A Child is Born, Lennart Nilsson. Dell, 1986.

A Good Birth, A Safe Birth, Diana Korte and Roberta Scaer. Bantam, 1984.

Becoming Parents, Sandra Sohn Jaffe & Jack Viertel. Atheneum, 1979.

Life Before Birth, Gary Parker. Master Books, 1987.

Positive Pregnancy Through Yoga, Sylvia Klein Olkin. Spectrum, 1981.

Praying For the Unborn Child, Francis & Judith MacNutt. Doubleday, 1988.

Pregnancy and Childbirth, Tracy Hotchner. Avon, 1984.

Right From the Start: Meeting the Challenges of Mothering Your Unborn & Newborn Baby, Gail Brewer & Janice Greene. Rodale Press Inc., 1981.

Transformation Through Birth, Claudia Panuthos. Bergin & Garvey Publishers, 1984.

Your Child's First Journey: A Guide to Prepared Birth From Pregnancy To Parenthood, Ginny Brinkley, Linda Goldberg & Janice Kukar. Avery Pub. Group, 1982.

Spiritual Principles:

A Course in Miracles, Foundation for Inner Peace, 1985.

As Of A Trumpet, Aumra. Foundation House Pub., 1968.

Beyond Belief, Lord Exeter. Foundation House Pub., 1986.

Handbook to Higher Consciousness, Ken Keyes, Jr. Living Love, 1975.

Meditations on the Lord's Prayer, Lord Martin Cecil. Foundation House Pub., 1982.

The Starseed Transmissions, Raphael (Ken Carey). Uni-Sun, 1982.

Inner Attunement:

Attunement with Life, Bill Wilkinson. Eden Valley Press, 1986.

Intuition Workout: A Practical Guide To Discovering and Developing Your Inner Knowing, Nancy Rosanoff. Aslan, 1988.

Opening to Channel: How To Connect Wtih Your Guide, Sanaya Roman & Duane Packer. H.J. Kramer, 1987.

Global Perspectives:

A New Science of Life, Rupert Sheldrake. J.P. Tarcher, 1983.

Earthrise, David Thatcher. Foundation House Publications, 1987.

Gaia: Humanity's Bridge from Chaos to Cosmos, Elisabeth Satouris. Aslan, 1989.

The Global Brain: Speculations on the Evolutionary Leap Into Planetary Consciousness, Peter Russel. J.P. Tarcher, 1983.

My World, My Responsibility, Michael Exeter. Foundation House, 1987.

Wholeness and the Implicate Order, David Bohm. Methuen Inc., 1983.

Childrearing:

Baby Exercise Book: The First Fifteen Months, Dr. Janine Levy. Pantheon, 1974.

How To Raise a Child of God, Tara Singh. Life Action Press, 1987.

Notes to my Children: A Simplified Metaphysics, Ken Carey. Uni-Sun, 1984.

The Well Baby Book, Mike Samuels, M.D. and Nancy Samuels. Summit Books, 1979.

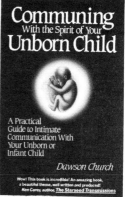

Francis and Judith MacNutt are well-known Christian healers and teachers. This book describes their rediscovery of God's love and power through their own experiences of pregnancy, and their growing awareness of the healing potential and sacredness of the event. With compassion and discernment, they list specifics to pray for at different stages of pregnancy, drawing on their wide experience of counselling parents through childhood traumas, abortions, and other issues.

Praying for Your Unborn Child, Doubleday, 1988 Item # 81-0 $12.95

An exquisite and authoritative exploration of the magic of prenatal bonding, <u>Knowing the Unborn</u> draws on the expertise of many of the best known researchers in this field, including Thomas Verny, M.D., Susan Ludlington, CNM, and the Prenatal University. A sensitive, moving documentary with scenes of birth and pregnancy, remarkable *in utero* photography, interviews with expectant parents and experts, with many practical "how-to" tips to encourage bonding from the earliest stages of pregnancy.

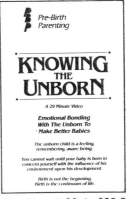

Knowing the Unborn VHS videotape, PBP Inc, 1988 Item # 22-1 $39.95

<u>Vision</u> by Ken Carey, modern prophet and author of the bestselling <u>The Starseed Trasmissions</u>, is a soaring vision of the possibilities open to the human race over the next few decades. Imbued with the spiritual principles which integrate the workings of cosmic patterns with human affairs, <u>Vision</u> is an inspiring manifesto of all that is possible as we claim our highest potential as a species. With a text that breathes hope, integration and inspiration, <u>Vision</u> is a powerful testament to the possibility of total renewal.

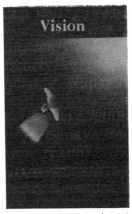

Vision, Uni-Sun, 1985 Item # 03-1 $6.95

Order Form

Title	Item	Price	Quan	Total
Heart of the Healer	12-9	$14.95		
Communing w. yr. Unborn Child (book)	15-3	$8.95		
Communing w. yr. Unborn Child (tape)	01-3	$9.95		
Intuition Workout (book)	13-7	$9.95		
(tape)	30-7	$9.95		
Praying for Your Unborn Child	81-0	$12.95		
Knowing the Unborn (videotape)	22-1	$39.95		
Vision	03-1	$6.95		

SUBTOTAL

CA. residents add 7% sales tax

Shipping: Book rate: $2 for first item, 50¢ ea additional item

First class/UPS $3.50 for first item, $1 ea add.

TOTAL check or money order enclosed

Your Name: _____ Mail to: Aslan Publishing
Address: _____ 310 Blue Ridge Drive
_____ Boulder Creek, CA 95006
Phone: (_____) _____ (408) 338-7504 or 338-2042

Order Form

Title	Item	Price	Quan	Total
Heart of the Healer	12-9	$14.95		
Communing w. yr. Unborn Child (book)	15-3	$8.95		
Communing w. yr. Unborn Child (tape)	01-3	$9.95		
Intuition Workout (book)	13-7	$9.95		
(tape)	30-7	$9.95		
Praying for Your Unborn Child	81-0	$12.95		
Knowing the Unborn (videotape)	22-1	$39.95		
Vision	03-1	$6.95		

SUBTOTAL

CA. residents add 7% sales tax

Shipping: Book rate: $2 for first item, 50¢ ea additional item

First class/UPS $3.50 for first item, $1 ea add.

TOTAL check or money order enclosed

Your Name: _____ Mail to: Aslan Publishing
Address: _____ 310 Blue Ridge Drive
_____ Boulder Creek, CA 95006
Phone: (_____) _____ (408) 338-7504 or 338-2042